In Their Own Words

The True Stories of Nine Buddhist Monks' Escape from Tibet

Scott 'Belmo' Belmer

LOTUS
PRESS

P.O. Box 325
Twin Lakes, Wisconsin 53181 USA

Page Layout & Design: Susan Tinkle

The photographs in this book were taken by Belmo, Terri Belmer and George Soister.

First Edition 2006

Printed in the United States of America

ISBN 13: 978-0-9409-8590-2
ISBN 10: 0-9409-8590-X

Library of Congress Control Number: 2005938432

Published by:
Lotus Press, P.O. Box 325, Twin Lakes, WI 53181 USA
web: www.lotuspress.com
email: lotuspress@lotuspress.com
800.824.6396

*This book is dedicated to all the peoples of Tibet
and their ongoing struggle under
Chinese occupation.*

Table of Contents

THE DALAI LAMA

MESSAGE

After Chinese communist forces entered Tibet and eventually took control of the country more than 40 years ago, understanding throughout the world of the tragedy that befell my homeland has grown considerably. However, what really happened, how the Tibetan way of life has changed and how people's personal hopes and ambitions have been crushed is less well known.

Therefore this collection of first hand accounts in which a group of young monks describe the fears and frustrations that continue to drive people to leave Tibet, brave the Himalayan passes and seek their fortunes in an unknown land is especially valuable. I hope that readers of *In Their Own Words* will not only be moved by these individuals' stories, but will also be persuaded of the justice of the Tibetan cause and will be inclined to give it their support.

October 20, 2004

An Introduction

*A*t the beginning of the new millennium, the Gomang Meditation and Dharma Center opened in Independence, Kentucky. Having a Buddhist study center in Northern Kentucky had been a longtime dream of George Soister and Hee Soon Choi. George and Hee Soon had searched for the right location for many months before coming upon an old schoolhouse in the quiet town of Independence. With the help of some friends they renovated the building and prepared their new Center for the first of numerous visits by several Drepung Gomang Tour Groups.

The first tour group arrived at the Center in 2001 and was kind enough to bless the fledgling Center. It was then that we were able to experience firsthand the teachings of Buddhism and to hear some of the monks' stories. The following year another tour group stayed with us at the Center. We shared meals, traveled to museums, colleges and local sights with the monks. Our daily contact brought us closer together and some special bonds were forged. It was at this time that the monks so graciously agreed to tell us their stories.

The interviews were held in the Dharma Room at the Center by George Soister and Scott 'Belmo' Belmer. The tour group's interpreter, Topten, translated our questions and the monks' answers. Each monk told us their stories individually. A few gave us detailed accounts of their lives, while others were a bit less forthcoming. Several of the monks were young and a bit shy about telling us about themselves. One of the monks, as you will see, spoke for over an hour with hardly any prompting from us. When we were done with the interviews, we found that their stories painted an amazing picture.

We had heard stories of the destruction of the Tibetan and Buddhist culture by the Communist Chinese during the past forty years, but we were unprepared to hear the horrors from the monks themselves. Through the tour's interpreter we inquired of each monk's background, tales of escape and life outside Tibet. It was an emotional several days for all of us as each monk related his personal account to us. Several of the monks broke down and wept as they told us their stories. Some of the monks are quite young and they still miss their families and the lives they left behind. They saw things that no civilized society should allow to happen.

We have kept their stories almost exactly as they were told to us. Grammar and punctuation was given a back seat to the expression of ideas, thoughts and memories in their own words. We felt in this way the reader would be closer to the monks and to the events that lead them to India and His Holiness the Dalai Lama. Emotions ranged from sadness, longing, happiness, anger, compassion, hope and loss. It was obvious that their faith was a great aid to their healing and their positive attitude.

These are the accounts of only nine monks. When one realizes that thousands of men, women and children have suffered similarly, it is nearly unfathomable that such destruction continues even today. But it does. Every day hundreds of Tibetans attempt to escape the Chinese oppression in their country. A few are able to make the difficult journey across the Himalayas. Many more are caught and imprisoned. Some are tortured or killed. And far too many die of starvation or exposure during that dangerous trek through the mountains.

Our intent with this book is to inform as many people as possible of the terror and inhumanity being perpetrated by the Communist Chinese Government in Tibet. Hopefully, people will be moved to speak out against the occupation and to assist financially the refugees in India.

*   *   *

As we were going to press with this book, we received this tragic news from Nepal where for years the Tibetan refugees (including those interviewed in this book) would receive aid before they continued their journeys to India. Where can the Tibetans turn to now for help? Here is the press release dated January 27, 2005:

Nepal closes Dalai Lama's office in Kathmandu
Agence France-Press
January 27th, 2005

Kathmandu - Nepal has closed two offices in Kathmandu associated with exiled Tibetan spiritual leader the Dalai Lama, Tibetan and foreign ministry sources said Thursday.

The government has closed the office of the Dalai Lama's representative and the Tibetan Refugee Welfare Office, a Tibetan source said.

"Following an official notification of the home ministry, we have shut down all the offices relating to the Tibetan refugees from this week," a senior welfare office staffer told AFP.

The welfare office looks after more than 20,000 Tibetan refugees who left their homeland after the Dalai Lama fled Tibet in 1959 amid a failed uprising against Chinese rule.

The Chinese embassy has frequently lodged strong protests with the Nepalese government for permitting the Tibetan office to operate in Nepal in the name of the Dalai Lama.

Nepal, which is careful not to antagonise its giant neighbour, recognises Beijing's rule over Tibet. A senior foreign ministry official said the Tibetan offices had not registered as required under Nepalese law.

The Tibetan Refugee Welfare Office (TRWO) had been helping several hundred destitute Tibetans who fled from Tibet across Himalayan passes to head to the northern Indian hill resort of Dharamsala where the Dalai Lama lives in exile.

After crossing into Nepal, the Tibetans are provided with travel documents by the United Nations refugee agency (UNHCR) to help them to travel to Dharamsala.

"The closing of the TRWO may be a big problem for the Tibetan refugees fleeing from the roof of the world for their political freedom," a diplomatic source said.

My deepest thank you to His Holiness the 14th Dalai Lama for honoring this book with His foreword. We are profoundly humbled by his recognition of the book and our intentions to aid the Tibetan monks and peoples in India and elsewhere.

I would like to thank the following people for their assistance in this book and for making the stay of the monks a pleasant and spiritual time: George Soister, Hee Soon Choi, Terri Belmer, Lobsang, the Wise family (Angeles, Haven and Talon), the members of the Gomang Meditation and Dharma Center, Migmar of the Drepung Gomang Monastery, Dgodup of the Office of His Holiness The Dalai Lama, the City of Independence, Cincinnati Public Library, Cincinnati Art Museum and a very special thanks to Angeles Wise for transcribing the interviews and his insightful editing.

And, of course, our sincere thanks to the monks of Drepung for sharing their stories with us. Their openness and spirituality is an inspiration to all of us. Additionally, their teachings of Buddhism and the examples of their lives have touched us spiritually and we are better people because of them. Thank you.

To make donations or to contact the Monastery:
Drepung Gomang Monastic Administrative Office,
P.O. Tibetan Colony-581411
Dist. Karwar,
Karnataka State.
India

Fax+91-08301-545697
Tel:+91-08301-545619/546084
Email: gomangoffice@yahoo.com
Web address: www.gomang.org

The Drepung Gomang Tour Group

Nine monks and an interpreter make up the Drepung Gomang Tour Group. The members of the Tour Group are carefully chosen from the Drepung Gomang Monastery for the various skills needed for their mission outside India. The members need to be skilled in the construction of mandalas, proficient chanters, dancers, musicians, cooks and communicators. Some knowledge of English is helpful but not required. They need to have the enthusiasm and commitment to participate in the project. And, of course, a willingness to endure the travel (and the hardships commensurate with long journeys in close quarters) required for accomplishing their goals.

In recent years the Tibetan Buddhist Monasteries in India,

(exiled from their homeland in Communist China occupied Tibet), have been sending touring groups of monks to the West to raise funds for operating and expanding their housing, educational, medical and meal providing facilities. This is necessary as refugees and orphans continue to stream into these monastic universities as they escape from China. Donations to the monasteries are given in exchange for Tibetan cultural performances, the creation of Tibetan art (the beautiful and intricate sand mandalas, or sand paintings), and the recitation of Tibetan Buddhist prayers for healing, happiness and world peace, in the famous "overtone" chanting to the accompaniment of drums, symbols, horns and flutes.

These are the Tour Goals as stated on the official web site:

> *To share compassion and the wisdom of Tibetan Buddhism.

> *To generate funds to insure the survival of this culture-in-exile. These funds will be directly utilized by the monks of the Drepung Gomang Monastery. They will be used to house, feed and educate everyone wishing to study at this monastic center of higher learning including orphans and refugees fleeing Chinese occupied Tibet.

The Tour Group is invited into communities across the United States and elsewhere to share their culture, traditions, and Buddhist teachings with the public. Often they are housed by Buddhist centers or individuals. The group members (and all of their costumes, instruments, Tibetan goods and personal items) travel together in one van. They may drive 10 to 18 hours at one time to reach their next stop on the tour.

Here are some of the things you might experience if you are lucky enough to attend an event by the monks:

The Tibetan cultural pageant features harmonic overtone

chanting of traditional prayers, accompanied by temple instruments including horns, flutes, bells, and drums. Delicate hand gestures and other offerings accompany the mystical rituals and multi-phonic singing, (each monk chants a chord of three notes). Richly costumed dances, including masked animals, will be performed. Together with the narration accompanying each piece and the monastic debate, the event provides a fascinating and warm glimpse into ancient and current Tibetan culture.

The creation of a sand mandala begins with an opening ceremony. Monks consecrate the site and call forth the forces of goodness through chanting mantras accompanied by flutes, drums and symbols. An outline of the mandala on the wooden platform is then drawn. The following days see the laying of the colors. The sand, colored with vegetable dyes or opaque temper, is poured to the mandala platform with a narrow metal funnel called a "chakpur" which is scraped by another metal rod to cause sufficient vibration for the grains of sand to trickle out of its end. The two "chakpurs" are said to symbolize the union of wisdom and compassion. The mandalas are created whenever a need for healing of the environment and living beings is felt. The monks consider our present age to be one of great need in this respect, and therefore are creating these mandalas where requested throughout their world tours.

The Mandala (Sanskrit for Circle) is an ancient form of Tibetan Buddhism. Mandalas are drawings in three-dimensional forms of sand. In Tibetan, this art is called "dul-tson-kyil-khor," which means "46 mandala of colored powder." Millions of grains of sand are painstakingly laid into place on a flat platform over a period of days. When finished, to symbolize the impermanence of all that exists, the colored sands are swept up and poured into a nearby river or stream where the waters carry healing energies throughout the world. When requested, the monks arrange to preserve a mandala, though this is not traditional.

The most common substance used in the creation of dul-tson-kyil-khor is colored sand. Other popular substances are powdered flowers, herbs or grains, and also powdered and colored stone. In ancient times, powdered precious and semi-precious gems were also used. Thus, lapis lazuli would be used for the blues, rubies for the reds, and so forth.

The subject for a Tibetan sand painting is known in Sanskrit as a mandala or cosmogram. In general, all mandalas have outer, inner, and secret meaning. On the outer level they represent the world in its divine form; on the inner level, they represent a map by which the ordinary human mind is transformed into the enlightened mind; and on the secret level, they predict the primordially perfect balance of the subtle energies of the body and the clear light dimension of the mind. The creation of a sand painting is said to affect a purification and healing on these three levels.

Every tantric system has its own mandala, and thus each one symbolizes an existential and spiritual approach. For example, that of Lord Avalokiteshvara symbolizes compassion as a central focus of the spiritual experience; that of Lord Manjushri takes wisdom as the central focus; and that of Vajrapani emphasizes the need for courage and strength in the quest for sacred knowledge. Medicine Buddha mandalas are created to generate powers of healing.

The monks are available to do blessings in private homes, convalescent homes, hospitals, offices, businesses or such public places as libraries or similar locations. The monks offer prayers wherever requested for specific purposes, or for a combination of blessings. Called "pujas," a Sanskrit word for worship, offerings are made and prayers are recited in the traditional overtone chanting, each monk singing a full chord of three notes. The prayers are often accompanied by delicate hand gestures, symbols, drums, horns and flutes. Prayers may be recited for a house blessing, the evolution of the soul of a friend or relative who has passed on, (including animals), the clearing of karma, pacification of local negative energy, world peace, individual or global healing, financial security, spiritual evolution, the development of wisdom, and the removal of obstacles.

Available Pujas:

- ·World Peace and Healing
- ·Purification
- ·House Blessing
- ·Removal of Negativities and Obstacles
- ·Tara and Guru Puja
- ·Tea Puja
- ·Fire Puja

The monks can perform a Tibetan Debate for the public. Debates are typically done at the monastery as a way for the monks to learn scriptures and Buddhist text. Debates are often quite lively and animated. In this lineage of Tibetan Buddhism, the Gelugpa sect, the gaining of inner wisdom through the practice of debate is highly honored. Monks of all ages spend hours in lively discussion at the large debate grounds, often way into the early morning hours. The monks' grasp of scriptures and textual reference is tested and honed. Though the debate itself is in Tibetan, the liveliness, joy, and spontaneity is infectious, and a translation of the general content is provided afterward.

The Tour Group members are also available to relate aspects of their life stories (as found in this book). The public can ask the monks questions and learn some details of the monks' lives while living in Tibet and at the monastery. The life stories of each of the monks are fascinating. Some of the monks were born in Chinese occupied Tibet and spent months traveling on foot through the snow-covered Himalayan Mountains. Sleeping outside and fleeing Chinese soldiers, they reached the monasteries in Nepal and India where they are free to study their own language, culture, and religion. Others, though born in freedom, have inspiring reasons for joining the monastery; some made the decision as young as age eleven. The monks are happy to share their stories, describe life in the monastery, and answer questions.

The Unity Celebration

East and West Reunified through Drumming, Dance and Chanting

"When the iron eagle flies and horses run on wheels, the Tibetan people will be scattered over the earth and the dharma will go to the land of the red man."

TIBETAN PROPHECY

"When the iron bird flies, the red-robed people of the East who have lost their land will appear, and the two brothers from across the great ocean will be reunited."

HOPI PROPHECY

One of the goals of the Tour Group on their visits to different parts of the world is to interact with indigenous peoples of the area. With this in mind we arranged for the Tour Group to meet with the local Mekoce Shawnee Indian Tribe on April 27, 2002. We thought it would be a wonderful and educational opportunity for the two groups to interact. After their initial meeting both sides agreed to gather for a musical collaboration on the Mekoce Indian Reservation located just north of Cincinnati, Ohio, at the Fort Ancient State Memorial. The gathering was open to the public and was held on a cool and rainy afternoon.

The monks brought along their drums and horns, while the Indians had their flutes and drums. Both, of course, had their unique singing and chanting voices. All were dressed in their traditional garb and the air was electric with their excitement. The event began with a procession into the holy meeting area. There were speeches of welcome and friendship on both sides. The monks opened with several of their traditional songs and chants – "Mandala Offering," "Mikt-

sema" and "Choed." Then the Indians performed some of their songs – "Flaunt Your Shawl," "Kiowa War Song," "Day n Day," and "Nonahe."

Finally, both groups joined together around the drum and chanted and sang together. These songs were "Nyur-

Zema/Cedar Song," "Trail of Tears," "Drums of Unity," and the rousing finale and crowd favorite "Yoey."

Members of both groups connected not just physically but spiritually that day – through their music, conversations, and just being in each other's presence. It was a joyous time and one that both sides loved and will always remember.

A Brief History and Relevant Information

Drepung Monastic University is a Tibetan Buddhist Monastic Institution that has been in existence since 1416 AD. It was the largest Buddhist University in Tibet and was founded by Jamyang Choje, who is the closest disciple of Great Je Tsong Khapa. Out of the two Monastic Universities under it, Gomang is one of them. At its zenith, Drepung Gomang Monastic University had over three thousand and three hundred monks, not only from all parts of Tibet, but also from Russia, Mongolia and other parts of the Himalayan region. This University has produced many eminent scholars, philosophers and mystics known throughout Tibet and its neighboring countries, who have revived the spirit of the Buddha's wisdom and messages of inner peace, compassion and non-violence.

After loss of sovereignty to China in 1959, a small group of 100 Gomang monks were able to flee to India with the goal of creating a Tibetan environment in which to preserve and maintain cultural identity and religion. With their own tireless labor, 60 monks finally succeeded in reestablishing Drepung Gomang Monastic University in the plains of South India in 1969. It was a very difficult time but thanks to the farsighted guidance of His Holiness the Dalai Lama, the monks have largely been successful in preserving their ancient Buddhist tradition.

Today there are more then 1500 monks studying at the University. About 150 monks arrive annually from Tibet, swelling the University's population. In 1998 there were 221 from Tibet alone. Children (some as young as six years old) and adults continue to flee Chinese-occupied Tibet to South India and arrive at the monastery penniless to study their own language, culture, and religion freely. Monks from India, Nepal, Bhutan, the Czech Republic, New Zealand, Mongolia, and Russia are also arriving at the monastery. The University provides facilities to everyone wishing to study the great texts in a monastic setting.

Study at the University is rigorous. Every year, six days a week, over 46 weeks per year, the students devote one hour for memorization in the morning followed by two hours of debate. After lunch, they have three hours of classroom and another two hours of debate. After dinner break, the debate practice will continue once again, sometimes stretching till morning. The traditional education of a novice starts from the memorizing of scriptures and learning of elementary texts. The mode of instruction is mainly through discussion or dialogue between the teacher and the student. A dialectical method of inquiry is used in these discussions. After more than 20 years of extensive studies in Pramana, Madyamika, Abhidharma and other related subjects, a monk is eligible to appear before the Gelugpa Examination Board. After finishing that he will be honored with the highly venerated Geshe

Degree (equivalent to the Doctorate of Philosophy in Western University).

Tibet: Geography and Relevant Facts

Tibet is located at the center of Asia, with an area of 2.5 million square kilometers. The earth's highest mountains, a vast arid plateau and great river valleys make up the physical homeland of 6 million Tibetans. It has an average altitude of 13,000 feet above sea level.

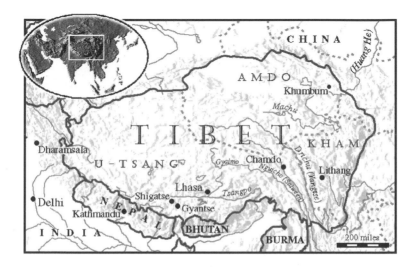

SIZE: 2.5 million sq. km.

CAPITAL: Lhasa

POPULATION: 6 million Tibetans and an undetermined number of Chinese, most of whom are in Kham and Amdo.

RELIGION: Tibetan Buddhism is practiced by 99% of the Tibetan population.

LANGUAGE: Tibetan (of the Tibeto-Burmese language family). The official language is Chinese after Chinese occupation in 1959.

STAPLE FOOD: Tsampa (roasted barley flour).

NATIONAL DRINK: Salted butter tea.

TYPICAL ANIMALS: Wild yak, Bharal (blue) sheep, Musk deer, Tibetan antelope, Tibetan gazelle, Kyang (wild ass), Pica.

TYPICAL BIRDS: Black-necked crane, Lammergeier, Great-crested grebe, Bar-headed goose, Ruddy shell duck, Ibis-bill.

MAJOR ENVIRONMENTAL PROBLEMS: Rampant deforestation in eastern Tibet; desertification, poaching of large mammals, and dumping of nuclear waste.

AVERAGE ALTITUDE: 14,000 Feet / HIGHEST MOUNTAIN: Chomo Langma (Mt. Everest) 29,028 ft.

AVERAGE TEMPERATURE: July 58°F / Jan. 24° F.

MINERAL DEPOSITS: Borax, uranium, iron, chromite, gold

MAJOR RIVERS: Mekong, Yangtze, Salween, Tsangpo, Yellow, Indus, Karnali.

ECONOMY: Tibetans – predominantly in agriculture and animal husbandry. Chinese – predominantly in government, commerce and the service sector.

PROVINCES: U-Tsang (Central Tibet), Amdo (N.E. Tibet), Kham (S.E. Tibet).

BORDERING COUNTRIES: India, Nepal, Bhutan, Burma, China.

NATIONAL FLAG: Snow lions with red and blue rays. Outlawed in Tibet.

POLITICAL AND RELIGIOUS LEADER: The 14th Dalai Lama. In exile in Dharamsala, India.

GOVERNMENT: Communist (after Chinese
occupation in 1959).

RELATIONSHIP WITH THE P.R.C.: Colonial

LEGAL STATUS: Occupied

1949–1951: The Chinese Invasion

China's newly established Communist Government sent
troops to invade Tibet in 1949-50. An agreement was im-
posed on the Tibetan Government in May of 1951, acknowl-
edging sovereignty over Tibet but recognizing the Tibetan
Government's autonomy with respect to Tibet's internal
affairs. As the Chinese consolidated their control, they re-
peatedly violated the treaty and open resistance to their rule
grew, leading to the National Uprising in 1959 and the flight
into India of the Dalai Lama.

Tibet in Exile

POPULATION (approximate)
Total: 142,000

India 100,000
Nepal 25,000
Bhutan 2,000
Switzerland 2,000
Canada 3,000
United States 10,000

GOVERNMENT: Democratic. Popular & electoral
college voting systems.

HEAD OF STATE: His Holiness the Dalai Lama

CABINET MINISTRIES: Education, Finance,
Health, Home Affairs, Information &
International Relations, Religion & Culture and
Security

INDEPENDENT COMMISSIONS: Tibetan Supreme Justice Commission, Tibetan Central Election Commission, Public Service Commission, Audit Commission

ELECTION SCHEDULE: Assembly & Cabinet elections every 5 years

SEAT OF GOVERNMENT: Dharamsala, northern India

INT'L GOVT. OFFICES: Budapest, Canberra, Paris, Geneva, Katmandu, London, Moscow, New Delhi, New York, Tokyo, Zurich

GOV'T PUBLICATIONS: Sheja (Tibetan), Tibetan Bulletin, News Tibet (English), Tibbat Bulletin (Hindi), Actualites Tibetaines (French)

INDEPENDENT PUBLICATIONS: Mangtso, Da-sar, Da-sa Phongya, Rangzen (Tibetan); Xizang Luntan (Chinese), Tibetan Review, Rangzen (English)

LITERACY: Estimated at 60%

MILITARY & POLICE: None

GOVERNMENT INCOME: Annual voluntary tax, business revenue, donations

NATIONAL FLAG: A mountain with snow lions & red and blue rays over sun

NATIONAL HOLIDAYS: March 10 – Uprising day; July 6 – Birthday of the Dalai Lama;

Sept 2 – Democracy Day; New Year (date changes)

MAJOR INSTITUTIONS: Institute of Performing Arts, Library, School of Dialectics, Medical Institute, Institute of Higher Tibetan Studies

TIBETAN NGOs: Women's Organization, Youth Congress, Amnye Machen

LANGUAGE: Tibetan. The host country's language is also spoken.

RELIGION: Tibetan Buddhism

ECONOMY: Agriculture, agro-industrial, handicrafts, small business, carpet weaving

LEGAL STATUS: Stateless. A small percentage of Tibetans bear foreign passports. Most hold Indian registration certificates.

Ten Quick Facts on Tibet

1. The nation of Tibet was invaded by China in 1949. Since that time, over 1.2 million Tibetans have died as a direct result of the occupation, over 6,000 monasteries have been destroyed, and thousands of Tibetans have been imprisoned and tortured for their political or religious beliefs.

2. The Dalai Lama, Tibet's political and spiritual leader, fled Tibet in 1959. He escaped to India along with over 120,000 other Tibetans, and established the Tibetan Government-in-Exile in Dharamsala. In 1989, he was awarded the Nobel Peace Prize for his steadfast dedication to non-violence.

3. Tibet was independent. Tibet had a sovereign government, currency, postal system, language, laws, and customs. Prior to 1951, the Tibetan government had signed treaties with foreign nations including Britain, Mongolia, and Nepal. While the Chinese Government claims that Tibet has always been part of China, its invasion of Tibet resembles the same imperialist aggression that China accuses other powers of exhibiting.

4. The "Tibetan Autonomous Region" is not Tibet, nor is it autonomous. Currently, the Chinese Government has divided historical Tibet into

many regions and prefectures. The TAR encompasses only the central area and some of the eastern regions of historical Tibet, and well over half of Tibet's original territory has been absorbed by Chinese provinces. "Autonomous" is a euphemism for direct control by Beijing.

5. In Tibet today, the basic freedoms of speech, religion, and assembly are strictly limited, and arbitrary arrests continue. According to human rights groups, there are currently over 1, 200 political prisoners in Tibet, including the Panchen Lama, imprisoned since age six. Repression in Tibet is currently the most severe it has been since the Cultural Revolution.

6. The Chinese Government's policies of forced abortions, sterilization, and population transfer of millions of ethnic Chinese into Tibet threaten the very survival of the Tibetan people. Chinese colonists outnumber Tibetans in most urban areas and many rural areas, making Tibetans a minority in their own nation. Meanwhile, thousands of Tibetans continue to flee from occupied Tibet, making the treacherous journey over mountain passes and into the uncertain world of exile.

7. Historical Tibet was a vast nation, whose area was roughly equal to Western Europe. Tibet is the source of five of Asia's greatest rivers that provide the lifeblood for 2 billion people. China has endangered Tibet's fragile environment through strip-mining, nuclear waste dumping, and extensive deforestation. Furthermore, Tibet's most sacred lake, Yamdrok Tso, is currently being drained for a hydroelectric power plant.

8. Although the Chinese government claims to have developed Tibet, most new jobs benefit Chinese colonists, not Tibetans. Tibetans have little or no say in how their country is developed. China

has spent millions of dollars building infrastructure in Tibet, but many of the roads, buildings, and power plants directly support heavy militarization of the plateau, allowing China to maintain Tibet as a police state.

9. China is aggressively seeking foreign investment for its new "Go West" campaign in Tibet and East Turkestan. China is trying to use international funds to develop Tibet as a resource extraction colony and consolidate control over the region. Foreign investments in Chinese companies give legitimacy to China's colonization of Tibet, and the exploitative projects they fund do not benefit Tibetans.

10. The world community has done very little to pressure China to improve its human rights record. China represents a gigantic market and cheap labor force, and its associated businesses have such a strong lobby in democratic governments that politicians are reluctant to impose any trade sanctions. Since western countries have recently adopted policies of "constructive engagement" with China, the human rights situation in Tibet has drastically worsened. Before this will change, world governments must take decisive action to pressure China into respecting human rights.

Information courtesy of Students for a Free Tibet

Two monks enjoy a quiet moment before the beginning of the
Unity Celebration with the Mekoce Indians.

The Drepung Gomang monks chanting at the opening ceremony
of the Unity Celebration at Fort Ancient in Ohio.

Prior to the creation of a sand Mandala, the monks begin with a ceremony of chants, mantra recitation and music blessing the site.

The monks begin the Mandala by drawing precise lines ("thigs") based on sacred geometry as written in the ancient scriptures.

Colored sand is applied to the Mandala with construction beginning from the center outward.

Millions of grains of colored sand are poured from metal funnels called "chakpurs" to create the Mandala.

After the completion of the Mandala, the monks chant prayers of dedication. Mandalas generally take three to five days to complete.

The monks work diligently on the sand Mandala as visitors to the Cincinnati Art Museum look on in fascination.

Thupten and Paljor put the finishing touches on the Mandala, which will measure about five feet in diameter when complete.

After the Mandala has been dismantled, the monks proceed to the
Ohio River where the sands will be dispersed as a blessing
for the universe.

To help raise money for the Drepung Gomang Monastery, the
monks sell Tibetan-made incense, tapestries, clothing and jewelry.

This is the Buddha of Compassion Sand Mandala, honoring "Lord Avalokitesvara." Its purpose is to encourage every one of us to generate a compassionate heart for the benefit of all sentient beings. It was created by the 2002 Drepung Gomang Tour Group.

As part of the Tibetan cultural event, the monks perform costumed dances. The masks and costumes are all made by the monks.

At the conclusion of the event, the tour group appears in traditional Buddhist attire as they play their horns, flutes, cymbals and drums.

The Interviews

Topten: Interpreter

My name is Topten and I was born in Bhutan in 1974. My parents left Tibet in 1959 when the Chinese Government took over Tibet. We moved to India in 1981.

I have one brother. He is a monk. Now he is working in the office of His Holiness the Dalai Lama. And I have two younger sisters. One works in the Office of the Audit Department of the Tibetan Government-in-Exile in India and one is studying nursing. My mother is 65 and my father passed away a few years ago.

My parents were farmers in Tibet. They grew barley, radishes and potatoes. They had yaks, goats and sheep. They were very happy living in Tibet. They had a simple life. But when the Chinese Government came in they destroyed the peaceful lives of everyone in Tibet.

Several years ago I studied business administration and I went to the Monastery on holiday. I noticed that the monks had problems because they could not speak English. So I offered my services for the two months I was on holiday. I was also very interested in Tibetan Buddhism, and I thought it was a good opportunity for me to help them and to learn basic Buddhist philosophy.

After my two months there I went back to college where I graduated. Later I received a letter from the Office saying they liked me and wanted me to come back. So I quit my job in Delhi and went to work at the Monastery where I have been for nearly seven years.

I worked at the school and as a secretary in the Monastery. We ran the library and a small handicraft school teaching traditional Tibetan handicrafts. It gives the people jobs and it gives them training so they can run their own business. We have a very small farm with 200 cows that provide milk for the common kitchen for the 1500 monks. We have a school with 180 students of different ages, and special classes for the older monks who want to learn English, science and math. For the last few years we have had teachers from other countries.

I attended the Tibetan Home School in northern India where I studied English. It is run by the Tibetan Government-in-Exile. Then I went to the Delhi University and studied English.

I came to the United States for the first time on February 2, 2002. Previously I had gone to Europe with some monks to share our culture and bring the peace and harmony message to the world and to raise funds for the Monastery in India.

We asked Topten about his impressions of the United States.

When we first came to America it was very different. As you know, Tibetan and Asian life moves slowly, but here people are so fast and busy. But too fast is not good and too slow is not good. Sometimes I think people do not have time to think about positive merit for the benefit of all human beings and all sentient beings. They are so busy that they do not have time to offer their merits to sentient beings.

Are Americans not as sensitive to the needs of their fellow humans as they should be?

Yes, but I have come across many people who are interested in Tibetan Buddhism. We have been to many states and cities. It is very important to have positive intentions and spiritual mind and heart. Because once you have that spiritual mind and heart, then you can have that positive intention to benefit other sentient beings.

Is there a hierarchy in the traveling group? What are the dynamics of the group?

We have two Geshe-las in this group. The one Geshe is Lobsang Tsetan. He is the leader and has a PhD degree. And the other is Geshe Lobsang Kunga. He has a Masters degree. "Geshe" means teacher - a teacher of the Buddhist philosophy. The rest of the monks are students. Some are in what we call high schools where they are studying. And once they finish their high schools of philosophy they will take their Gelugpa Exams. And they study for six years and they will get a Geshe degree. To get a PhD degree they must study for 21 years.

It is different for us to get a degree. We do it to get a better job or something like that. For the monks the higher degree means they can study more, practice more, experience more. Once they finish their degrees some monks continue to teach what they have learned to the younger monks. Some monks go out of the monastery to isolated places for retreat. Now they want to practice what they have learned. Buddhist philosophy is not something like metaphysics. It is more important for them to practice patience, or meditate on the nature of reality or how to practice compassion. As soon as they finish their studies they go to the forests or the mountains on retreat.

But some monks go into retreat for the rest of their lives. There are two traditions of Buddhism: Mahayana and Hinayana. For the Mahayana practitioners, their main mission is to try and help other sentient beings. They are trying to reach the state of liberation or of enlightenment. Once they reach this state they are free from the three basic delusions. Their mind is free from hatred, attachment and ignorance. Once their mind is free from these delusions, we can say they have reached the state of liberation where they can find blissful happiness.

When they have reached that state they can come back to the human existence (the samsara) in order to help other sentient beings whose minds and hearts are troubled by the basic delusions. From these delusions we do the negative things. Samsara is the cyclical existence. There is no beginning and no end.

What are the difficulties and the positives of ten men traveling together in one van?

Most of the monks came from Tibet and have experienced very hard lives. When they left Tibet they crossed the high mountains of the Himalayas. So for them, when they travel in one van, it is very easy. Sometimes for me it is difficult – especially when we travel for 16 hours or so. At the same time, before we start our trip, all the monks start chanting to remove the obstacles and to remove the bad luck along the way. So I try to chant with them and to think on the words and to concentrate on the powerful energy of their chants and prayers. They are not only praying for themselves but for the benefit and welfare of all sentient beings. They are always offering their merits for the benefit of others. So they are not only praying to remove the obstacles for the monks in the van but for all of society.

The monks are very happy. But when they face some small problem, they try to visualize the suffering of all sentient beings. When they do that, they consider their suffering as very little. In that way we come up with positive reactions from our minds and hearts.

Whenever we have a long trip ahead we cook our lunch early in the morning. We always have our lunch at a rest area. We sing together and have fun. Sometimes we share our stories and jokes and try to make fun.

You recently performed at Carnegie Hall. What were your impressions of that event?

The Tibet House in New York organized that event. We met many different artists and we don't know how famous they are. We met David Bowie, Patti Smith and many other artists and great thinkers. To the monks they are just ordinary people. We had a good time. Those artists are very good and are concerned about the Tibetan people.

What are your impressions of performing with the Mekoce Indians at Fort Ancient in Ohio?

It was the best time I had since being here in the United States. The Native Americans are very exceptional – their culture is quite ancient. I noticed there are many similarities between the two cultures. The Tibetans are trying to preserve and share our culture and the same with the American Indians.

I know very little about Native Americans and had never met any in my life. I was moved by their culture. Their way of preserving culture and our way are very similar. One is the incense we use and the smoke sticks they use to purify and bless their performances and the people.

When we were drumming together I noticed that the monks really had a good time. In our tradition our instruments are sacred. We offer the music to all sentient beings and the meditational deities. It is the same with the American

Indians. They consider drumming to be very important and very sacred.

Finally, we get a lot of support from the Americans. They are aware of Tibet and the situation. We appreciate the support. We are trying to get the basic human rights. Not to benefit ourselves, but to get peace on Earth. And we want to give the message of love and kindness and compassion to the people of the world.

Gyaltsen Tharpa

M y name is Gyaltsen Tharpa. I was born in July 1973
in Kala in central Tibet. It is high mountain country.
When I left Tibet I was 23 years old. I had become a monk in
1989 – three years before I left Tibet. My parents are still in
Tibet and I have two older brothers and one younger sister.
I became a monk at the age of 18. My parents are Buddhists
and I am the only monk in the family.

I am able to talk to my family on the telephone and I also
send letters. In the year 2000 my parents came to visit me
in India.

My family's condition is not too bad now, unlike when
the Chinese first went into Tibet. There was much trouble.
Now my family can conduct their business without much

Communist Chinese interference. They can farm now but must pay taxes. And since my family lives near the border with India, the Chinese allow them a certain amount of freedom to conduct their business.

All the top members of business (such as doctors) are paid by the common people who must pay part of their income to the Chinese Government.

When I was 23 I went to Lhasa (the capital of Tibet) by bus to Kala and to the Nepal border where I walked on foot for 18 days. There were six of us traveling together – five monks and one lay person. When we crossed the border we found a way to cross to Nepal. During those 18 days we had a problem with food. We were running out of food. But our problems were not as bad as those who had to cross the high mountains of the Himalayas. So our group was lucky to find a reasonably easy way to cross the border.

Then we walked to the village of Kala and we tried to cross the border. During the daytime we would hide in the thick forest because of the Chinese troops and the Nepal border troops. What we had to do was hide and sleep during the day and at night we walked in the forest. It was very difficult, but at the same time it was safer.

When we reached Nepal there was a place called the Reception Center where we were cared for. At the Center we were asked where we would like to go – monastery or school? I wanted to go to the monastery. There were many refugees there suffering from frostbite – including many children. They told us many terrible stories.

How did you come to be a part of this group?

I was chosen to be a part of the group because I am a good chanter. I like it very much. I had been to Europe a few years earlier on a tour with other monks, so for this tour the office at the Monastery requested me because I had been on tour before.

I enjoy traveling with this group and meeting the people

of America. Americans are so open-minded and openhearted. The people in Europe and the people in America are very open and frank. It is easier for me to be with the Americans than the Europeans.

When we were in Philadelphia in February we took a trip and we saw the Guinness Book of Records and I had not seen anything like that. I can't imagine how these things are all real. I was amazed by the man with horns and the man whose ears hung very low. It surprised me that things like that happen.

We asked if there were any places in America that he would especially like to visit.

There is no special place I'd like to see, but I enjoy going to different places because I can meet different peoples and see different cultures and ways of life. Wherever I go I gain new experiences and that helps me a lot.

But that is not why I am here in this group. Because our culture is being destroyed by the Chinese Government, we are trying to preserve our ancient culture and to make our culture aware with the people of the world. And we are trying to bring peace and harmony to the world. Plus we are trying to raise funds for the 1500 monks at the Monastery. This is the main aim of our group.

What did you think of your experience with making music with the American Indians?

When I see all the Native Americans while we did the music together, I imagined the day we will get our country back. When we played the Flag Song and the Native Americans had their flags too. I imagined all those Tibetans still in Tibet and I go back to see them all in my mind. I feel that Native Americans have all the opportunities and the equal rights and religious rights in America. But the Tibetan people have no equal rights and no political rights. I wish the Tibetan people still in Tibet could experience these kinds of rights.

I have one thing to share with the Americans about the current situation in Tibet. In Tibet since 1959 when the Chinese Government took over, there have been no human rights in Tibet. Even in the monasteries in Tibet the monks are not allowed to put pictures of His Holiness the Dalai Lama in their shrine rooms. It is very sad.

In Tibet the Chinese Government is building railroad tracks into central Tibet. The main reason is that the Chinese are trying to transfer their population into Tibet. Now there are more Chinese than Tibetans in Tibet. And then they are taking the natural resources and moving them to China. Their main aim is to try to bring more Chinese into Tibet and to extinguish the Tibetan culture.

In Tibet the Chinese Government controls the births and if Tibetans have more than three children they have to pay the Chinese Government money for each child more than three. And they force sterilization and abortions of Tibetan women. In that way the Chinese are trying to replace Tibetans. And also the Chinese soldiers are forcing young Tibetan women to have sex. It is a terrible thing.

The Panchen Lama was six when he was taken from Tibet and no one knows where he is. Or if he's alive or in prison. There are many organizations trying to gain his release but it is not working.

The main reason I am sharing my story with you is that I want each and every person of the world to try to get justice for the Tibetan people and try to get our country back. We want to gain peace and human rights in Tibet. We want to thank you for supporting the Tibetan cause.

What are your plans after your tour in America is completed?

After the tour finishes I'll go back to India to the Monastery and continue my studies. I will have missed my studies for one year because of this tour. My main aim is not to just obtain a higher degree. I want to try and train my mind to experience the real peace. From the Buddhist point of view

– especially the Mahayana Tradition, we are always trying to benefit all sentient beings. But here I want to help sentient beings through my training and experience. At least with those around me, I hope my experiences and my Buddhist philosophies will help them.

Thupten Monlam

My name is Thupten Monlam. I think I was born in September 1969 but I do not know for certain. My home was in Nagchu. My parents and family live in Tibet. I have one older sister and two younger sisters and three younger brothers.

In 1989 I escaped from Tibet by crossing Mount Kailash in the Himalayas alone and on foot. Once I reached Nepal I joined with several other monks. I had left Tibet with only 50 yen and I soon ran out of money and food. I had very little clothing. It was a very hard journey. I had to beg for food and shelter. No one would give me tsampa, but some families gave me potatoes.

From my home in northeastern Tibet it took me seven days to reach Mount Kailash. I walked around Mount Kailash for a year as part of my pilgrimage. Mount Kailash is a Tibetan holy mountain. Then from there it took me three days to walk to the Tibetan border. I traveled during the spring and summer of 1989.

Once I reached Nepal I contracted chicken pox and became very ill. No hospitals would help me or give me medicine. I was homeless and was ill for over a month with chicken pox. Then I met an old Tibetan man at Kailash in Nepal who took me in to his home and kept me from dying.

I studied and became a monk at the age of 14. My parents didn't want me to be a monk but I wanted to be one. I studied at a small monastery in Tibet. The Chinese set limits on the number of monks in our monastery. Just 200 were allowed. The Chinese forced the excess to leave the monastery.

My typical day began at five a.m. and would start with pujas. Sometimes I recited the scriptures in the Buddhist texts. I would do this until nine a.m. From nine to eleven a.m. I would memorize scriptures or go to the teachings at the monastery. We had lunch from eleven to twelve.

After lunch I'd continue memorizing scriptures until five p.m. Then at five I go to classes to learn how to memorize and do the sacred rituals. It was a small monastery so we did not study the philosophies. We studied until nine p.m. and then ate dinner. After dinner was finished we would go to our rooms to sleep.

We asked how he was chosen for the group.

I was asked by the Head Office of the Monastery to be a part of this group. I have no special talents.

The interpreter told us that Thupten's chanting is exceptional and that he is a chant master. Thupten was just being modest. He is also very good at drumming and playing the long horn. He learned the long horn while in India.

This is my first trip to the United States. I had been to Europe several times. I enjoy traveling with the group but sometimes there are small disputes and different views. Also, we are very busy and we don't always eat on time.

When I return to India I will continue my studies. I'd like to come back to the United States someday. I hope that with your support, Tibet will be free again someday.

Paljor Tsogngon

My name is Paljor. It means 'wealth'. I was born in eastern Tibet in the Tsognon province. It means 'blue lake'. This is a mountainous area in the Himalayas.

I have one younger and one older brother. My youngest brother is a doctor in Tibet. Since the 1960's and 1970's my parents and our family had a very hard life under the Chinese. The Tibetans had to hide their wealth from the Chinese. They told the Tibetans in the 1970's that we'd be free, but we were deceived and the Chinese took everything from us.

My parents were farmers and nomads. But in the 1970's the Chinese said all were equal, so they took from the rich and were supposed to give to the poor. But they kept it all for themselves.

I became a monk at the age of 13. I had to attend a Chinese school until I was 13 years old. They taught us the Chinese ideology and that Buddhism was not good. They only taught Tibetan for one hour a day. The rest of the time was studying Chinese ideology.

At age 13 I decided I didn't want to study Chinese. So I went to the monastery to study Buddhism, but there wasn't much opportunity because the Chinese forbade many of the teachings. I knew about the Dalai Lama in India and I knew I must escape Tibet and receive his blessings in India.

One of my cousins was taken by the Chinese and put in prison for a long time. The Chinese killed thousands of monks, nuns and other Tibetans for no reason.

I escaped Tibet in 1990 to meet the Dalai Lama. And I wanted to study the Kalachakra Teachings in India. The other reason I left was that I knew very little about Tibet except that there were no human rights in Tibet for Tibetans.

When I reached India at the age of 17, I learned about Tibet and its history. And I finally learned Tibet had been a country for thousands of years. In Tibet there is no history of the country taught. Most young Tibetans know nothing about their own country because the Chinese only teach their own ideology. For instance, even if you say "Free Tibet", you will be put in prison. And you can't show the Tibetan flag.

On the way to India I crossed the Himalayas. I traveled with two other monks. We were from the same monastery in Tibet. We had about 500 Chinese currency. By the time we reached Lhasa we were out of money. But, fortunately, we met a man in Lhasa who gave us about 60-70 Chinese currency. With that money we bought some food and drinks.

Then we started our journey to India.

It was at this point in the interview when Paljor had to stop because his emotions overwhelmed him. He continued a few minutes later.

Because we are very young, we miss our parents.

Sometimes we met some Tibetans who gave us money to buy food. We were traveling on foot and we had many hard times along the way. Sometimes we had to beg for food. Many nights we slept on the streets in towns or on the ground in the forest. Often we slept in caves or at the bottom of the mountains.

The most difficult part of the journey was the time we tried to cross a very huge river in the winter. In order to cross that river there is a small bridge there. But the bridge was guarded by Chinese soldiers. So we had to go downriver to find a place to cross. And because it was winter, there was much ice in the river. It was very difficult to cross and the ice cut our legs and we were all bleeding badly.

After that it took us two days to cross the mountains. The wounds in our legs were still bleeding badly and it was very painful. We had few clothes and we were very cold. Along the way we saw many bodies of Tibetans who had died of starvation and the cold. We saw one person who had died standing. He was high up in the Himalayan Mountains.

Then after some time we reached the Nepal border. As soon as we could we bought butter because we could not afford medicine for our wounds. We applied the butter on our wounds to stop the bleeding and heal the cuts.

Fortunately, we made it to the Tibetan Reception Center in Nepal and those people were good and they helped us. They cured our wounds, gave us food to eat and clothes to wear. They also bought us bus tickets to go to India. We went to the Monastery where we met His Holiness.

I saw His Holiness the Dalai Lama. There were about 40 of us who went together. In that group were also my friends. We were the youngest ones there and we were allowed to sit in the front row. As soon as we received his blessings, I was very happy in my mind. The happiest I have ever been. He then asked us where we were from and why we left our homes. And then he blessed us. Because we were the youngest, he advised us to continue our studies and to join the Monastery.

Now it has been ten years since I've been at the Monastery. The Monastery sees to all our needs. Most of the monks who go on tour have a special talent or have completed their studies. But in my case I have all the necessary documents so I am asked to join the group. Also, I feel the responsibility to do something to help the Monastery. I know many traditional dances and songs of Tibet and that is why I was chosen to join the group.

When I was in India I heard many things about America. That it was a big and rich country. Everyone has the equal opportunity here to do what they want. And the traffic rules here are very good – unlike the traffic in India.

I am very happy in my group and I like to work together with other monks. Whenever we make the Sand Mandala or our performances, we always work together and make fun and make laughter. The most difficult part for me is whenever we travel for 16 to 17 hours – it is very difficult because I am not used to it.

Like the Native American culture, the Tibetan culture is in danger. Everyone must try to work hard to preserve these ancient cultures.

As soon as we finish the tour we'll go back to India. I'll continue my studies. I have been away for a year. Some time after I have finished all of my studies and obtain the Geshe degree, then I might come back to America and learn about modern education or maybe share my knowledge with the world.

I have a special interest in learning the Christian philosophies. I read about many Christian groups that try to help society. I want to learn about many different philosophies.

I would like to say to the leaders of the world to look into the truth of Tibet and other small nations. You will know that Tibet was an independent country for many years. Try to promote peace and give the people basic human rights. No matter what kind of religion or what race, I request that all leaders of the world to work together for peace.

As an ordinary monk and our group, we always try to pray to help promote peace on Earth.

Dhamchoe Phuntsok

My name is Dhamchoe Phuntsok. I was born in the Kham area, which is in the northeastern part of Tibet. And I was born in the year... I was born on the 15th of April. I am not very sure with the year. I think I am 30 years old.

If you could tell us about your family, if you have any brothers or sisters, if your parents are still living, and where they are right now.

My parents, they still live in Tibet, and I have four younger brothers. I am the eldest brother. One of my brothers came to

India in the year 1990. But I went back to Tibet last year. The reason I went back was because I missed my parents and my country, so I decided to go back. But, since I did not have any papers or travel documents, I was caught on the border by the Chinese troops and imprisoned for a few months. At first I was caught in Shigatse, which is a small city in Tibet, which is near central Tibet. I was put into the prison in that area for one month. After that I was transferred to another prison. Then they kept on transferring me to other prisons. In total, I have been in more than ten different prisons in Tibet.

The Chinese troops don't let me talk to the other prisoners. If I talked to other prisoners they would beat me and they never let me talk about the Tibetan Government-in-Exile. And they never let me talk about His Holiness the Dalai Lama to the other prisoners. In the prison I only received, once in a day, a bowl of rice with no vegetables and a cup of water. That was the only food I was fed in a day.

My brother also had been arrested when he came back from India because the Chinese troops think he might be some sort of spy of His Holiness the Dalai Lama. He had spent a few years in India in the Monastery of His Holiness the Dalai Lama. My brother was with some other political prisoners and then finally they transferred me to the same prison in the northeast part of Tibet. My parents went to the prison and tried to release me. Fortunately they were able to release me, my brother and his son. But at that time, my mother told me, she could not recognize her son because he became so weak, health poor, and he looked sick because the Chinese troops in the prison beat him and they treated him badly in the prison and he only got a bowl of rice and a cup of water.

Just a few days ago I called my mother on the telephone. I called from here to Tibet, and talked to my mom. She told me each and every story in detail.

The main reason why I escaped Tibet is that I was sent to India by my father. My father does not like the Chinese Government. So he finally requested me to go to India and to take part in the Monastery and also to follow His Holiness the Dalai Lama. Another main reason is because my father's real brother was killed by Chinese troops. He was deliberately killed by Chinese troops while in prison. How it happened is that one day while he was having a meal with his family, suddenly some of the troops came to his house and dragged him and put him into prison. After about seven days his family received a letter from the Chinese prison that they had already decided to kill him. They had given him a death sentence.

Then the Chinese government called all the family members and also his grandfather and grandmother and their parents. During that day they were forced to come to see their son (my uncle) while they decided to kill him. They wrote out a huge sign in front of him and attached it to his body, they put some bamboo poles in front of him, and then right in front of their naked eyes, all the families, the Chinese troops just shoot a bullet in the backside of his head, just killed him on the spot. So, that's why my father always advised me, try to escape Tibet and try to go to India under His Holiness the Dalai Lama.

The main reason for killing him was that during the 1959 and late 1950's, when the Chinese troops came to occupy Tibet, my father's brother was a very brave and a very strong man and he was in one of the groups to kill all the Chinese troops and he killed about thirty Chinese troops. That's why he got the death sentence. Also, soon after they killed my father's brother, they also tried to catch my father and imprison him. During that time my father was only twenty years old. As soon as he noticed the Chinese army or military going to catch him he left his home and went to some other places for five years. After five years my father came back to his home.

When did you leave Tibet? And what were the circumstances like on your journey to India?

I left Tibet in the year 1990. My younger brother also left after one month. When I left my family, when I left my country, most of my family did not know whether I leave or not because my father sent me to India. On the way of escaping I didn't face any special or any harsh circumstances except on the way because when you cross the border you always walk in the middle of night and during the daytime you just try to hide in the thick jungle or forest. On the way the worst thing that happened to me was for three or four days I was running out of my food. I had a very hard time. I had a very terrible time.

And my worry is that the Chinese Government might put my younger brother into the prison once again, because just recently when I talked to my mother and relatives on the telephone I heard that in our village the Chinese Government kidnapped the head of the village monastery and also the senior monks. I'm always worrying about my younger brother because he was once in a prison and they might try to put him into prison once again.

Were you a monk when you left Tibet or did you become a monk after you got to India?

At that time I just became a monk when I left Tibet.

How long did it take you to reach India?

When I reached Lhasa, which is the capital city of Tibet, at that time it was in the month of April. When I reached India it was in the month of July. So...April, May, June, July...almost four months.

When you reached India was there a group of people who helped you and assisted you and then did you continue your studies?

As soon as I reached India I met up with another group - other refugees. We all were taken care of by the Tibetan Reception Center in Delhi and Dharamsala. They gave us food, they gave us clothes, they gave us some money, as pocket money, and then finally we decided to go down to the southern part of India where the Monastery is situated to continue my studies. Actually, my father told me to tell the story of his brother to His Holiness the Dalai Lama and try to get the blessings for my father's brother. But I was unable to approach His Holiness the Dalai Lama and could not get the opportunity to tell my story to His Holiness the Dalai Lama. But, I visualized that His Holiness the Dalai Lama had blessed my father's brother.

How were you chosen for this tour group?

I've been working for the Monastery for the past few years. In the Monastery we have a special group called the special chanting group. I was in that group for the last few years and am told I am very good in different kinds of chanting. And I am skilled in making the Sand Mandala. That's why I was chosen to be in this group.

Had you been to the United States before or had traveled to Europe before with the group?

No, this is my first time to the United States.

Any impressions about the United States? Anything that you found was amazing or very interesting?

I've had many kinds of different experiences since I got to the United States. The first this is that I find that all the citizens of this country they have 100% human rights. They are open and they have every rights. Back in Tibet we don't have the religious rights or the political rights or the human rights also. As soon as I got to this country I thought that all the citizens of this country are lucky because they can do whatever they wish and that is good. Another one is that the

Americans are very open, and as far as I'm concerned, they are friendly to the monks and I really appreciate that. Also I noticed that there are many organizations that support Tibet and Tibetan people cause and that is also appreciated.

What do you like about traveling with the group and maybe something you don't like so much about being on the road?

I'm very happy with my group. Whenever I am in India I'm very happy with the other monks. I'm friendly to other monks. And even in this group, most of the monks are good to me and I'm very happy with the monks. I like traveling with the group like this, but one thing is that sometimes my mind just comes up with all the things that happened to me and my family in Tibet under the Chinese occupation, and sometimes when we travel for long distance my mind thinks about all those sufferings that we experienced under the Communist Chinese Government. At that time I feel kind of bad – so sad.

The day before yesterday I was playing with the monks and we were having a very fun time, but suddenly I decided to call my mom in Tibet. I got to talk to my mom and she asked me when I was coming back to Tibet to visit her and my family members. I told her that maybe I would try to come back to Tibet after three years. That very moment my mother she keep on crying and crying. And she just can't speak any words after that. Again, the rest of the day my mind was full of tension and worry about my mom and my family. Otherwise I'm very happy here.

What was your impression of the Shawnee Indians and of making music with them?

When I met all those Native Americans the other day I noticed that there are some minorities in this country. And they are striving to preserve their culture, which is very good. And at the same time I thought about the Chinese Government trying to banish away all of Tibet and Tibetan culture from Tibet. My mind was thinking about how it might be possible for the Tibetans that someday there will be no Tibetans and Tibetan culture in this world. At the same time I really appreciate their way of preserving their culture, but on the other hand I just thought in my mind that it might happen to the Tibetans soon. It was quite tragic for me.

We believe in our hearts that the Tibetan culture will not disappear. The Chinese will not destroy it as long as we have Tibet in our hearts and we continue doing what we can to preserve the Tibetan culture.

Thank you.

Thank you very much, Dhamchoe, for sharing your story and thoughts with us.

Ngawang Tashi

My name is Ngawang Tashi. "Nga" means your speech and "wang" means powerful. My name means I have a very powerful speech. That is one of the qualities of Buddha. "Tashi" means good luck. Together it is 'powerful speech with good luck.'

Great name...great name! As he knows, my name is Belmo. It means short, bald guy.

(Laughter from the monks.)

If you could tell me where and when you were born?

I was born in South India. The district name Mysore. Our village is named Gurupura. Gurupura is a small town that has many different villages. I was born in the village M on November first in 1978.

Did your family live in Tibet and then they went to India?

Yes, my parents are from Tibet. And my father has a former wife. When my father escaped Tibet he was forced to leave his wife and children in Tibet. When he reached India he married my mother. I have five brothers and one younger sister. Two of my brothers are also monks. There are three monks in my family.

I entered the monastery to become a monk when I was three years old. I have been there for 23 years. When I was three years old my father died and my mother had three small children to look after. And then my teacher (who was a very good friend of my late father) picked me out of my family and took me to the Monastery and helped me to become a monk. It was very hard for mom. She already had several children to look after. Things have been hard for her. My teacher also made my two brothers monks. There were about five other children there also.

At that time the Monastery didn't have many children. They don't have many small monks in the Monastery. And of course I was only three years old. They don't give any special lessons or something like that. Because at that time there was only one class for the small monks. The teachers only taught the Tibetan calligraphy or Tibetan handwriting. So, that's the only lesson we can learn in the Monastery as children. Then my teacher decided to put me into one of the village kindergartens. They teach the basics. I spent two years in that school. And then I was taken care of by one old woman who is a friend of my teachers.

When I was very small and in the Monastery, we do not have a special school. There is only a small group of students, so the teachers only teach one Tibetan text, which is called Lek-shey-jon-wang. Then in the 1990's, the Monastery built a school for the small monks. In that school we are able to learn some English, some mathematics, and social science, and also we are taught about the general science and the environments, in addition to the Buddhist philosophies and the Tibetan language and history.

What were your favorite studies? What do you enjoy studying the most?

When I was in school my favorite subject was history. At the same time I had a very big interest in learning the different kinds of environments.

When and how were you chosen to be a part of this traveling group?

This is my second visit to this country. I was in a culture tour in the year 1998. It was the first tour group of Drepung Gomang Monastery. And then I was also requested to join the second tour group, which was taken place last year. But at that time I decided not to join the second group. In the Monastery I'm in the class Prajnaparamita and in my mind, right from the beginning, I really want to study. You know, like seriously.

Because I had just started that class called the Prajnaparamita. If I missed that year it is sure that I would miss another one. I had decided not to miss my classes and I don't want to miss my classes. That's why I didn't join the second group. And now this is the third tour group and how I was chosen is like in each tour group there should be one Chant Master, which has a very low and deep voice. The Chant Master who was in the second group, whose name is Geshe Tashi, you might know him. As soon as he came back to India the monks elected him as the Chant Master of the whole Monastery. And of course he doesn't have time to be in the third tour group to travel because he is the Chant Master of the whole Monastery. And there is another monk who is very good and has a very low deep voice. The time with him is difficult because he has a lot of things to do in the Monastery. There were another two monks, but they went back to Tibet. Now the responsibility came on my shoulders again and the Monastery asked me to join the third group. That's why I'm in the third group.

When you chant, I notice as you sing you put your right hand in front of face/mouth, palm down, fingers together and extended pointing away from your body. What is the purpose of that?

There are several reasons. When I lead a chant, I use my hand like that *(makes same gesture with right hand)*. The first reason is that we use our hand and that we put our hand in front of our mouth just to lead several special chanting. We don't do that to lead every chanting. When we finish one chant and start another chant we don't, unless it is a special chanting then we do it. Otherwise we don't do it.

Another reason is that in Tibet, in one hall or monastery, we have thousands and thousands of monks. Whenever we start the chant it is to make sure that everybody can see the Chant Master. The Chant Master has the special throne and everybody (especially the monks who are sitting in the back side of the hall so that they can also see the Chant Master) know when to stop and know when to start another chanting. That is why I use my hand.

And the third reason is that in Tibet we don't have special facilities, like microphone and all these things. This is to spread the vibration of my voice. Because when my voice hits my hand, the vibration spreads and then each and every monk can hear what kind of chants I am leading.

There's also a saying in Tibetan Monastery Society that in Tibet all the Chant Masters became Chant Masters at a very old age in the Monastery. Some of the Chant Masters, since they are of very old age when they raise the chant, they have a really hard problem with their jaws. This is to give support to their jaws. This is just a saying. *(Everybody laughs.)*

At this point of the interview Ngawang demonstrates how he uses his hand during a chant.

This sound is very unique when you study on the deep and low voice. Each low voice has different levels and these are very special levels. We do this level during important religious ceremonies or religious festivals. And this chant is unique to the Gelugpa sect. We do this especially during the prayer festival of the Gelugpa sect. When we do this very low and deep voice, we produce three different tunes - three different notes at the same time. And we take the breath from our stomachs.

What kind of training did you take to learn how to chant like that?

It took nearly six years to come up with a very deep and low voice. When I was small and in the monastery the number of monks is very small. During that time the elder monks are very strict when we do the chanting and they are very strict on the different tunes of the chanting. Because the monks believe that the tune of the chanting is very important. And we should not mix up the different tunes when you do the chanting. They give a lot of practices to the small children to do that kind of tune and to produce that kind of a tune.

When I was small I always practiced and tried to produce this low and deep voice and sometimes I think that in the room when I practice it I disturb other neighbor monks, so what I do is I try to go to the field or somewhere to practice. Sometimes I practice while walking or while roaming with my friends. I always practice. In that way my voice has improved.

What were your impressions with making music with the Shawnee Indians on Saturday?

When I was small, as I mentioned earlier, I studied Social

Studies. In my subject Social Studies we learned different cultures and different people and I remembered that I also learned a little bit about the Native Americans - the Native Indians. I have always been eager and have had a segment in my mind to meet and to see that kind of a culture and to meet those people in real.

During the first tour in California some of the organizers held a World Festival. In that World Festival the tour monks were invited to join the World Festival and we met many different cultures of people and saw different traditional dances, different cultural performances - especially the performance of the Native Americans in California. So that time my mind is fully satisfied.

I think it is a very good opportunity for me to perform with the most ancient cultures or ancient people, the races of ancient culture. I always think it is a very great honor, pleasure, and at the same time it is kind of exciting to be performing with them Because we perform together in order to preserve peace on earth, in order to preserve this very kind of ancient culture on this earth. This is very exciting for me and I always appreciate the ancient culture.

And last Saturday when I was given the opportunity to drum with them, I thought it was very lucky for me and they are kind, they are open, and they are good. They are friendly to the monks and I appreciate that. I think that was the result because I was always eager and excited of meeting these people - the Native Americans - and other different cultures. When I was drumming with them, I liked that special song which is called "Yowee Yowee." Each and everybody were given an opportunity to sing. I was lucky to be with them and I thought I have laid down causes in my previous life to meet with them and I had a very good time with them.

What are your plans after the tour is over?

My main mission, even when I was small monk (I don't have a very big mission or huge aims and ambitions) but my mission as a monk is to be a sensitive human and try to become a Geshe, to obtain a Geshe degree, and also at the same time at this moment for the past six years I have been preparing for the role of Chant Master. So my mission is to become the Chant Master of the whole Monastery. That was my second mission. And my first mission, as I have mentioned, is that I want to be a sensitive human and when I finish my studies I want to practice all the Buddhist philosophies - what I have learned in my life. That was my mission.

Thank you very much. Thank you for sharing your stories with us and Ommmmmmmm!! (laughter)

Geshe Lobsang Kunga

Please tell us your title and your name.

My title is "Geshe," and my name is Lobsang Kunga. The meaning of "Lobsang" is "good heart" or "good soul." "Kunga" means "everybody loves" or "everybody likes."

I was born in one of the Nomad families in the eastern part of Tibet, which is called the Tso Ngongpo - the "Blue Lake." I was born in the year 1964 in the month of November. And I don't know the date because for most of the old Tibetans the date is not important. We don't know how to keep the dates. Including myself, my mother and father have nine children (brothers and sisters). I am the eldest one.

When I was a little boy I was raised in one of the Nomad families until I was about five or six years old. I did not know anything about what was going on in Tibet. But I do remember when I was about five or six years old at that time all the belongings, all the cattle, and all the material possessions that my family possessed, we were forced to contribute (give) it to the Communist Chinese Government.

My grandfather, he is a very special man, because in his body he can welcome the other deities. And through his body and through his mouth that particular deity can speak and protect the people. That's why the Communist Chinese Government they consider him as a very evil man. We had a hard time with the Chinese Government. Unfortunately he was caught by the Chinese Government. And they dragged him to some place and they beat him. For three days he could not take his breath. But he was not dead – he was still alive because his body was warm. After three days he was able to breathe again. I don't know this for myself. I heard this story from my parents. They consider my Grandpa as the reincarnation of God. In his previous life he was a God from the God realms. He has a very special and strange things happened in his life. He can also invite the deities and the other Gods into his mind. Those deities can speak with other people through his body, while using his body, his mind, and his speech.

There's always strife from Chinese troops. Whenever there are some problems or whenever there's suffering or sickness, in Tibetan tradition you would always go to the person like this and request him to invite the deities and figure out what has happened to that sick man or what are the causes of that problem. What he does, since there is strife from the Chinese Government, he always helps other people by inviting the deities into his mind in the middle of the night, sometimes one o'clock in the morning, two o'clock in the morning. In the middle of night he tries to recite many prayers and do some chantings, and then he would invite the deities into his body. Sometimes while he was sleeping he could talk as if he was awake because all those deities came into his body and all those deities are talking to the other people. Whenever he invites the other deities into his mind, what other people do is burn the incense, a lot of incense, and they try to remove all the evil and the bad spirits from his body – like the Native

Americans.

And then he has special dress. As soon as he puts on this special clothing the consciousness of his mind comes with that particular deity. And also we are supposed to give him some rice or barley to bless it. What he does with that uncooked rice or barley is very interesting. On his right hand he holds a very sharp knife, the deities are in his mind and he cuts his tongue and produces a lot of blood. Then he mixes that blood with the barley or uncooked rice and he gives it to the sick people to heal their body or whatever it may be. It really works and it does help. And as soon as the deity goes away from his mind then there are no scars or wounds on his tongue.

And also I remember that my mother was sick for a long time. And one time she was very bad. She was seriously ill and she was lying on the bed for many days. Then in the middle of one night my parents invite him to our home to do the blessings, the healing and things. And then what he does is he took a knife and he cut the breast of my mother from here *(left side nearest the heart)*.

I can clearly remember this, though I was very small. I can see a big hole where he cut my mother's breast. You can see a huge hole inside. At that time, because I was very small, I was scared and very worried about my mom. I woke up really early the next morning, since I was scared and worried about my mom. I went to my mom and asked her what happened to her and that wound. Then I saw just a scratch – there's nothing there! Just a scratch is there! This is something that I saw through my naked eyes. This is really amazing! I don't know if people believe this or not, but I saw it with my naked eyes.

That's why the Chinese Government regarded religion as a poison and they especially hate the people who are religious – like my Grandpa who has the deity in his body or does these kinds of things. They are especially stressing or focusing on these types of people. That is why the Chinese Government people do not like my Grandpa. And also, my Grandpa didn't like any of the Chinese Government people.

That's why he never used Chinese clothes or Chinese hats, because most of the Tibetans during that time some of them they use the Chinese hats because they got them at a very cheap price. But he never used the products made by Chinese or produced in China.

Also he is putting efforts to keep our culture alive. He's always appreciating the ancient culture of Tibet and is always advising all of us to preserve this ancient culture very proudly. Whenever we listen to the radio about the Chinese news, he doesn't like us to do that. One day he heard from some of his friends that Mao Tse-Tong has died. He was happy with that news that he borrowed some Chinese currency from some of his friends and then he went to the market and bought a small radio. He paid forty Chinese currency just to listen to that news. *(laughter)*

At that time all the Tibetans were supposed to tie a black piece of cloth here *(around the left bicep)* and also the small children are forced to attend meetings. In the meetings they talk about all the qualities of Mao Tse-Tong and all of the Tibetans are forced to pay homage and respect to Mao Tse-Tong. They were always announcing that he's a very good man and he did such and such good to Tibet and for Tibetan people. They are just trying to educate people with that ideology. Each and every Tibetan is forced to tie a black piece of cloth here *(around the left bicep)*. As soon as we get home, since my Grandpa does not like anything about Chinese activities, we had to keep it away from the eyes of my Grandpa. This is a big story about my Grandpa. But, my father, he is a very simple man. He's not like my Grandpa. He's just an ordinary being. *(laughter)*

I spent almost seventeen years as a Nomad with my family. And now I am thirty-eight years old. Sometimes, when I look back to my childhood life, I think that I was really lucky to be born in a Nomad family because even though we don't have many facilities, like normal families, the people who are Nomads they are very peaceful and friendly to each other, and we experience happiness all the time. When I look back to my childhood, my early life, I feel very happy.

The main reason why the Nomads are very happy is that they are very happy with their cattle - all the animals. They treat their animals as something very precious and they totally depend on their animals. They are very happy with their animals. Another reason is since the Nomads are always busy with the animals they don't know anything about the politics or the issues or anything about the things going on in the world. For them, even if the world has a problem, they are happy people because they are ignorant. They don't have any idea. That's why they spend their lives peacefully and they are very happy.

They totally depend on those animals. They regard their animals as the precious ones for them. For them, when they feed their cattle, if the valley is not good and it rains too much then this is a big problem for them.

During the summer season as Nomads we built small bamboo houses in Tibet. When it rains it comes into there and everything is wet. Since we do have lots of sheep, goats, and other small animals there is a danger of fox attacking the sheep and goats. That's another problem with Nomads. Their main food, since we live in very high mountains, is meat, butter, cheese, and milk. The products of the animals are the main food for the Nomads.

If they had a very beautiful day when the sun shines then they try to find some other beautiful place. Where there are many places for the cattle, they make their bamboo houses again. They keep searching for places. Every season they go to different places. During the summer season they go up on the mountains. And in the winter season they come down and live in the valleys, because it is too cold up there. And in the spring season, because it is such a beautiful season, a lot of grass is coming out and is green, so again they go to different places.

I remember during the spring and summer season we see many different varieties of the beautiful flowers. All the flowers bloom out and there are many beautiful different kinds of birds singing in the forest. I miss these in my life. Here in this country I notice some of the same flowers that grow in Tibet. There are some flowers that even grow in this country. My family has four hundred sheep, seventy yaks, about twenty horses, and some other small animals. I remember when I was small we would ride on the horses and we would do horse races. I remember all those good days.

Most of the time, when I look back at my childhood, I think that I'm very lucky to be born in a Nomadic family. I spent my childhood in a very peaceful environment. But on the other hand, sometimes I feel regret that I spend my time like this as a Nomad. Why? Because I didn't get the opportunity to study and I didn't get the opportunity to educate my mind. Sometimes I feel regret.

During the wintertime all of the Nomadic people come down to the town because it is too cold up there in the mountains. We just come down and I remember that I attended classes. These were not schools, but a group of people from whom you can learn some letters, how to write, how to read. Only one hour in a day. And then every year in the wintertime my family sent me to that group of people to learn how to read. Finally, I think I spent five years learning, like what you would to go into the fifth grade.

When I was sixteen years old I saw a monk for the first time. It was during one of the Tibetan New Year gatherings. In Tibetan tradition what we do on the first day of the Tibetan New Year (That is called Losar. Losar means "New Year."), we go to different families and try to visit each other. At that time I saw a monk and I felt so peaceful and I felt a very different state in my mind. Then I decided in my mind to become a monk. I told my parents I wanted to become a monk, and they let me become a monk. They are kind. And that monk I met became my teacher. He was a kind man because he always came to the village to help the ordinary people.

When I told my parents I wanted to become a monk, my parents told me that there is no place to study to become a monk in our village. Much of the time of the year is spent up on mountains and they are Nomads. There is no place for the monks to do their studies. Fortunately, that monk, that Geshe, is a very kind monk. He decided to take me with him and he led me to become a monk in his monastery, which is called the Ku-bhum.

At that time I had turned seventeen years old. Once I reached the monastery I found out there are rules and regulations made by the Chinese Communist Government. One rule is that nobody is to become a monk unless he is eighteen years of age. Again I had some problems because here I was only seventeen years old. In that monastery there are about sixty monks and all the monks are of very old age. There were no young monks.

I would like to make one thing clear - the reason why the Chinese Government made this rule. In the schools no Tibetans are allowed to become monks until they are the age of eighteen. The main reason is that in the schools they teach Communist ideology. They turn their mind into the Communist. Once they reach the age of eighteen their mind is already developed with Communist ideology and they consider Buddhist religion as some kind of poison. I was lucky. Because I was a Nomad and didn't have any ideology of Communist Government, I became a monk.

I remember in my parent's home we had a small altar. Also, we had some pictures of His Holiness the Dalai Lama, the picture that depicts his visit to China. Since my parents know nothing of the political issues, they are just very religious. They have deep faith in His Holiness the Dalai Lama. That is why they keep a portrait of His Holiness.

Even in these days there are many young Tibetans who don't know anything about Tibet. Even though they are Tibetans and live in Tibet they don't know anything of Tibet, Tibetan religion, and Tibetan culture. Most of them don't know the Tibetan flag or the Tibetan national anthem because of the Chinese in the schools. One thing everybody knows is His Holiness the Dalai Lama and the Panchen Lama who is the second highest spiritual leader of the Tibetan people.

I was only seventeen years old. So because of the rules and regulations by the Chinese Communist Government to that monastery, I was not allowed to become a monk. I had to spend one year passing my time in the monastery trying to help the monks. And because I was not a monk, I was not allowed to wear monk's clothes and I had to wear casual dress for one year. At that time the monks were repairing their temples, repairing their prayer halls, repairing the whole monastery because the Chinese Government destroyed everything. You could see the damage done by the bombs and bullets.

When I went to the monastery, which is called the Ku-bhum Monastery, the monks were repairing their monastery. I remember I had to spend my time in that monastery. Because I could not become a monk, I devoted my whole time to help the monks repair their monastery. I remember I always carry lots of supplies on my back up to the second floor. I helped the monks to repair the temple. And the huge temple that is in the middle of that area once had rooms for the monks. But all the rooms were destroyed by the bombs and explosions of the Chinese Government.

I spent one year like that - helping the monastery to repair. Then in the month of April, according to the Tibetan calendar (it is a very precious day for the Tibetans according to the Buddhist tradition) at that time I had turned eighteen and I was allowed to become a monk in that monastery. So finally I became a monk in the month of April. I became a monk along with twenty new monks. Once we became monks at the Ku-bhum Monastery, we had to take some sort of transfer documents from the Chinese people. I had to go back to my parents' home and get all the paper documents. Because the Chinese Government keep all the records on who became a monk. They keep track of all these things. I went back and told my parents, took all the papers, and then came back to the monastery.

Again I had very big problems when I went back to my parents' home to get that letter, to get that approval letter. I remember there was a Chinese policeman who had this document. He denied issuing me that document because I was small, even though I had just turned eighteen. He did not believe me because I was very short at that time. He didn't believe me and denied to me that document. At that time I was angry. I spent one whole year in the monastery as an ordinary man. I had turned eighteen and still they are denying me - they are not ready to issue me the transfer documents. If I don't have that transfer documents then again they are not going to allow me to stay in the monastery because each and every person should be registered to the Chinese people.

I had to argue with that Chinese policeman. I remember I told him that you cannot tell other people's age from the size of the body or something like that. Finally, after one month, he showed me that transfer document. And then I became a monk at that monastery. I studied Tibetan language and also the Tibetan Buddhist philosophy for almost six years in that monastery.

When I first got into the monastery I had some problems because I missed my Nomadic life. I missed my parents. As a Nomad boy I can go everywhere. But in the monastery I cannot do that. As a Nomad I didn't know anything about these things. I had some problems before I could get used to it.

But even in the monastery, since the monastery has no authority to give the education opportunity to the monk students because of the Chinese Government. The Chinese Government made many new rules and regulations for the monastery. Even in that monastery I don't get much opportunity to study. And sometimes, whenever there are some visitors from another country or from the Tibetan government, what they (Chinese officials) do is send message to the monastery and tell us to have the lessons or to gather together for the puja. They are pretending that they are giving the opportunity for the monks to practice our religious activities.

On the other hand, I was quite lucky. My teacher was a very kind man. He's a true practitioner and since he considered me as his student, I always try to get the good qualities that he possessed. That helps me. He was very smart because when he was young he went to the Sera Monastery – one of the three main Tibetan monasteries in the central part of Tibet. He told me the whole history of Tibet and other political situations. I remember that every evening he would teach me all these things. I also remember that he taught me many things about His Holiness the Dalai Lama - how a group of people searched for him and picked him up as the true Dalai Lama. I remember all those stories.

And finally, because there are no religious rights in that monastery, my teacher advised me that it is best for me to go to India where there are human rights. Where there are individual rights. Where there are political rights. Then my mind changed and my teacher advised me, even though in Tibet those three big monasteries are still there, but they are already destroyed and there are no religious rights, even in those three big monasteries in Tibet. That's why he advised me to go to India and continue my studies. He always told me this indirectly. He never told me directly that "Oh, you should go to India." Again, because I can understand what he means, whenever he advised me he advised me indirectly. He advised me to go to India and continue my studies. That was in 1985.

One of the elder monks came back to Tibet from India to meet my teacher because they were friends when they were young. They were in one of the same monasteries. That old monk came back from India to Tibet to visit my teacher. He spent seven days in our monastery. He told us each and every thing about the three big monasteries in India, about the religious rights, about the facilities, and that you have the opportunity to learn the Buddhist philosophies. He told us every thing in detail. He told us about the Tibetan Government–in–Exile and also he told us about the culture of teachers that was supposed to happen in 1985.

And he told me that there are many people from America and many people from different parts of Europe who were helping the Tibetan Government-in-Exile. That was the first time when I realized something about the Tibet situation. Also I learned a little about the Tibetan political situation. Our teacher has about sixty students, so everyone has to go through a history of Tibetan teachings. One day I have some friends, about the same age, and since we heard all the stories about India, and then finally we decided to escape and go to India with some of my friends.

One night I was sleeping and was thinking about planning to go to India and then suddenly I have a second thought that if I go to India it's so far, I would surely miss my family members and friends, especially my teacher. He was old and if I go to India, who is going to take care of him? I worried. But then I decided to go to India. At that time I decided in my mind, so I told my friends I was not planning to go to India because of my parents and because of my old teacher.

Then after six or seven days I was not feeling very good, and again my mind is coming up with these second thoughts. And the third thought that "Oh, it's better if you go to India to continue your studies." At that very moment I realized that it could be what we call my karma, the karmic action, or even if I have to think about my teacher and think about my parents the causes and karmic situation comes on me. So I decided to go to India. Even though I have many friends, many close friends, I never told them that I'm planning to go to India because it's not a very good idea. But I have two other friends, including myself we are three, we always for the few days have been planning how to do that. How to take the trip to India. And I remember that we had been planning and trying to get some money for our trip. Then I told a lie to one of my friends, 'I'm just going back to my hometown to meet my parents', and I told him to look after my teacher because at that time he was quite old. I told a lie to one of my friends and I ask him to look after my teacher.

I sent a message to my parents and said I was supposed to do some special religious ceremony. In that ceremony I had to do a demonstration of the debate. That's why I sent a message to my parents to come down to the monastery to witness, to bring some money, and to bring some food. My parents showed up with some money, some food, and they came down to the monastery to attend the ceremony. During the ceremony I prayed and offered money to all the monks in the monastery and I made some offerings to the Buddha.

I prayed to all the monks because I had to go to India. I

have only two reasons I decided to go to India. The first reason is to get the blessing and to meet His Holiness the Dalai Lama. And the second reason is to continue my studies. I heard that there are individual rights and equal opportunity in the monasteries in India to continue your studies.

Then I told a lie to my teacher. Usually he gives me all the keys to the doors and boxes, and we have a few boxes and the door keys. I keep all keys with me. One morning I went to my teacher and told him the lie that I'm going back to see my parents. I'm going back to the Nomad area. Then I gave him all the keys in his hand.

At that time I was preparing to leave for India. My parents had come down to the monastery to attend the ceremony. I told my teacher that I'm going back with my parents for at least fifteen days or maximum of one month. I told my teacher that after one month I would come back to the monastery. Along with my two other friends and my parents, we left the monastery. Then we proceed towards the town called Selene and that was the day that I departed from my monastery.

When I departed from my teacher I considered him as my guru - my own teacher. That moment was the saddest moment of my life. As soon as we reached that small town called Selene, I told some lies to my own parents and I had some belongings that I'm trying to hide because we are planning to go to India. Then I went with my parents to home and spent six to seven days with them. And I did some prayers. I did some special prayers along with my parents and then I left. During the six or seven days I spent at my parents' home I read the whole text of The Path to Enlightenment as a prayer for my grandmother. I told a lie to my parents that I was going back to the monastery. My parents gave me a bunch of butter, cheese, and some money. And instead of going to the monastery, I went to that small town called Selene where my other two friends were waiting for me. They were also planning and ready to escape from Tibet. We went to the place where we hide some of our belongings and we took them back.

From Selene we went to Gyaimo. That was the first time that I rode a train. We took a train from Selene to Gyaimo. We had a very good time on that train because we had cheese and curd with us. Once we reached Gyaimo we bought a bus ticket from Gyaimo to Lhasa. That bus belongs to a Chinese company. The bus was supposed to leave early the next morning. As soon as we woke up we went to the bus. When we got to the bus we took our own seats, because there's a number on the tickets. But some of the Chinese showed up and they tried to kick us away from the bus. The bus company people gave our seats away to other Chinese.

One of our friends (he's quite strong) and I went to the bus office. My friend started beating that bus officer from whom we bought our bus ticket. They are a little bit afraid and they told us that they were sorry but they cannot give us seats. They gave our seats to the other Chinese and other tourists. They treated us like that. We decided not to stand on that bus because we are angry and not very happy with the people who treated us so poorly. We tried to get our money back. Finally we got our money back, took back all our luggage, and we took another bus to Lhasa. The driver of the other bus was Tibetan. He knew we were monks so he gave us seats at the front of the bus. We were very, very lucky.

After two days and one night we reached Lhasa which is the capital city of Tibet. We had a little bit of a problem with the language, because the Tibetan language we speak is from the eastern part of Tibet. The accent is totally different from the people who speak Tibetan in the central part of Tibet. But luckily we met many good people, many kind Tibetan people who live in that area. They took us into the palace of His Holiness the Dalai Lama, which is called the Potala Palace. They showed us his room, his offices, and everything. They took us to visit all the historical places, the pilgrimage places, and they showed us each and everything in that town. I saw the images of Songtsen Gampo the King for the very first time. He was a good and famous king who brought the Buddhism from India to Tibet. He was a great king. His name is King Songtsen Gampo. We went to get blessings and we went to see a huge Buddha Shakyamuni statue – what we usually call as Jowo (located in Lhasa at Jokhang Temple).

For the Tibetans this is precious and something very important. I got the blessings from that statue. There is a saying that everybody is saying in front of that huge statue of Buddha Shakyamuni, which is called the Jowo. If you pray and if you tell your mission to him, it will help you to fulfill your dream or he will make it so. I offer some butter lamps and I prayed that I would be able to go to India to get the blessings from His Holiness and to continue my studies. I prayed to remove all the obstacles on the way to India.

We spent about seven days in Lhasa. After seven days we proceeded to the village Tashi Lhunpo (in Shigatse). As soon as we reached the village Tashi Lhunpo, we met three other Tibetans who are from the northeast areas of Tibet. They had a compass. Those three Tibetans were also planning to go to India. We made our own group and we started our journey. There we brought many Buddhist texts. But once we reached the Tashi Lhunpo, we realized it's not possible for us to take them with us. We always walk. It is too heavy to bring all those texts on our back. We had decided to leave all those texts with one older monk in the monastery. We did not sleep in the guest room of that monastery because the Chinese Government kept a record of all the guests in that guest room. What we had to do was sleep outside the monastery in the courtyard. After that we started our journey.

In the middle of the night we started our journey, because during the daytime it's not possible. After walking for about seventeen days we finally reached the Himalayan ranges. Most of the time we slept during the day and walked during the night. One night when we were walking when there suddenly was a jeep. In that jeep were three Chinese troops. They stopped in front of us and asked where we all were going. We told a lie. We said we were planning to go on a pilgrimage to the Mt. Kailash. We consider Mt. Kailash to be a pilgrimage place. Since they were Chinese police they knew that this was not the way to Mt. Kailash. They told us it's better to go back because this is not the right way to the Mt. Kailash. Then we decided to go back a few yards. They didn't catch us. They sent us back from where we came from.

We did not follow that road because there were many Chinese police. We took another road during the daytime and the nighttime. After a few days we reached a very small town that was quite near to the border of Nepal and Tibet. We spent some time with the local people of that town. We told them that we are going to India and they started helping us and they showed us the right way. They told us that if we follow on that particular path that there are many police and they will catch you. They showed us another way which is quite difficult to cross. That way is on the high mountains. There is many ice and snows that it is difficult to cross. But that is the best way to cross - away from the Chinese police. We had some money so we bought some tsampa. As you know the tsampa is the flour of the barley. We bought some tsampa to eat on the way and then we again started our journey and we tried to cross that very high Himalayan Mountain.

It took us almost two days to cross that very high mountain. Most of the monks, most of the people, in our group were the Nomads and we were used to climbing high mountains. But one of our friends is not a Nomad and he's not used to climbing such high Himalayan mountains. He had a very terrible time. He had a lot of pain on his leg. He had a very terrible time. But I carried all his luggage with my own luggage to try to help him.

Finally after two days we crossed that high Himalayan Mountain. It was very difficult. When you are on the peak of the Himalayas it is very difficult to breathe. When you reach the peak or on the top of the mountain you feel kind of dizzy because of the air. If you eat garlic it's really helpful. Sometimes in Tibet we eat various kinds of grass or other plants that have a strong smell. And if you feel dizzy you try to smell that plant. It helps. We had a very hard time up on the mountain.

We spent one day in the snow trying to climb that high mountain. Because the mountain is sloped like this (acute an-

gle) and the sun is shining from this side *(other side)*. All the snow is like ice – very hard and difficult to walk on the snow. The mountain is steep, so it is very difficult. But one of our friends who is from the Kham area, he is a very strong man. He is leading our group and trying to find us some way to cross. It took us one day to cross that Himalayan Mountain. As soon as we cross the top of the hill we tried to go down the mountain. Since there was sunshine all the ice and all the snow started melting. Then it's very difficult when you are trying to step on the ice and snow. You sink down and there's ice under the snow. We had a terrible time.

One time I was stuck in very thick ice and my right leg went into deep snow on the mountains. I tried to pull out my leg but then my left leg would sink into the ice. It took me a few hours just to get out of that ice. At that moment I thought, "Oh, I'm going to die...I'm going to die." My mind and my eyes filled up with tears and regret because now I'm going to die in this snow mountain and I should not have done this because I told a lie to my teacher and I told a lie to my parents. Now I'm going to die in this snow because my body is exhausted. And I can feel that my body is cold. I cannot get out of this snow because there is so much snow and ice, and I keep going deeper and deeper in the snow. And I thought that "Oh, now I'm not able to get the blessings from His Holiness the Dalai Lama or go to India. I cannot make my trip to India." I felt out of control and hopeless.

My other friends tried to pull me up from this snow. But when they tried to pull me up, they also got stuck in that snow. Also, I have a lot of luggage on my back. It made me very heavy. One of my friends told me to pull off all of the luggage. Half of my body was in the snow. So I pulled off all of the luggage and gradually I was able to keep my mind in control and to get out with the help of my friends.

This is another lesson I learned from this experience. When you are stuck in the snow, it is always the best way to come out of the snow if you have a blanket or whatever, a huge luggage, just kept it like this in front of you and put your hands like this and try to come out with the support from that luggage.

Then what we have decided that if you step, if we walk, it's very difficult. If you do like I did sometimes there are huge holes and you might just get into the holes of snows in the mountains. What we had to do, instead of walking, we lay down and rolled like a ball. If you roll down it is much easier. So everybody tied their luggage very tightly on our backs and we rolled down like a ball. After about half an hour of rolling and rolling down, we then felt some thorns and rocks. We are now at the bottom of the snow mountain.

We now felt we were safe and we are at the bottom of this snow mountain. It was between spring season and summer season and the rays of the sun were quite hot. There was an avalanche that's coming down from the mountain. I can see that. It was falling down on our heads.

I tried to jump out of the way. The moment I jumped that whole area went down. The size of the avalanche was as big as this hall. The other side of the ice was coming out and rolling with the ice and the snow. I thought I am going to die because of the ice and that avalanche. So I visualized His Holiness the Dalai Lama and I prayed for him to help.

It was funny because with the ice it was as if I was ice skiing. It was moving down and it's quite far away. The mountain was like this (very steep slope) and I was on the ice and because the size of the ice is very huge and I'm not rolling. But luckily I soon reached the bottom of the mountain. It didn't injure me or anything. I was fine. I reached the bottom of the mountain. I was lucky to be alive. Then I looked back and all my friends are still up on the mountains. I am the first one who reached the bottom of the mountain. I walked about twenty minutes far away because it is not very good at the bottom of the mountain because of the avalanche.

I took out some kerosene oil that was in my luggage. I made some tea while waiting for my friends to come down. It took more than one hour for them to get to the bottom of the mountain. Finally, everyone made it down and we had a cup of tea. It was in my mind as I went down with the ice and the snow that I was just going to die. It did not seem possible that I was still alive because the mountain was so steep and so far away. *(Note: We later found out that this mountain was Mt. Everest!)* I was falling down with the ice and snow, but still I'm alive. I visualized and prayed to His Holiness the Dalai Lama from my deep heart.

A few years later His Holiness the Dalai Lama visited our monastery and kept the teachings on the Path to Enlightenment. Thousands and thousands of monks attended the teaching. Then, suddenly, among the thousands and thousands of monks, he recognized me and looked at me and smiled. He smiled at me! I believe that I had been protected by His Holiness the Dalai Lama. I have very deep faith in him. When I was falling down with the ice, I visualized him and he protected me. I believed that he knew my situation and that's why he recognized me among the thousands of monks and he smiled at me. That makes me happy. That's why I have deep faith in him that he's always trying to protect the Tibetan people and the people who are suffering.

When my friends reached the bottom we had tea together and relaxed for a few hours. Then we resumed our journey. We saw a huge rock with something written on it. Later some people told us that it was the border of Tibet and Nepal. Once we crossed the Nepal border we came upon a small monastery. We spent almost three days in that monastery.

By then we had run out of food and had to buy some more. In that region the food is very expensive. We bought some tsampa. For this much of tsampa they charge one Chinese currency, which is very, very expensive. To get some money to buy food, I decided to sell a valuable animal skin that my parents had given to me. It's a very good shirt. I sold it to some Nepalese for 170 Nepalese rupees. The cost of that shirt is about two hundred Chinese currencies.

Also, we bought some yellow beans. We weren't used to eating beans as we eat only tsampa and butter tea. It was quite difficult to taste the beans when I first ate them. After about two days we had eaten all of our tsampa. We had some old tsampa. When we have new, fresh tsampa, we don't touch the old one. But since we are running out of our tsampa, we had to eat that old tsampa. In English it is what you call moldy or fungi. It was delicious because we are all hungry and we don't have any food to eat. I realized that whenever somebody asks me, "What is your favorite food?" I always remember that situation, that moment, and say whenever I am hungry, that whatever I am eating during that moment, then that is my favorite food. That was the most delicious one. But since we were all very hungry it was delicious and I never will forget that delicious tsampa.

That's why when I was small I remember my parents always when I tried to eat some tsampa. And if I throw some tsampa away my parents always caught me because they had a bad experience. They had a hard time in 1959 when the Chinese troops came into Tibet. During that time thousands and thousands of Tibetans died from starvation. No food at all. I remember the advice given by my parents. When I was small if I throw away a piece of bread they always caught me. They considered that food was precious and is the product of many other beings' efforts and hard work. That time I realized that was really good advice.

We had nearly run out of our food, but fortunately we crossed into Kadari where some Nepalese farmers grow potatoes. We stole some potatoes from their field. We were hiding and stealing potatoes. We put all the potatoes together and made a small fire and we fried the potatoes on that fire. We found a small sack so we could bring the rest of the potatoes with us and we started our journey once again.

After that village there was another very huge and deep mountain. But it was not a snow mountain. We had to cross that mountain once again. When we reach the top of that mountain, even though there is no snow, it is all foggy. We can't see our own way because it was foggy on that mountain. We started eating the rest of the potatoes that we have cooked. We put all the potatoes together on the plain rock. The potatoes were fully mixed up with the mud on the rock. We eat mud and potato all together. That was very delicious, even though it was a mixture of the mud and the potato...so delicious. Fortunately on that mountain there are many strawberries. We picked many strawberries and ate everything. We spent a whole day on top of the mountain and we ate all the strawberries and the potatoes and mud and everything.

It began to get dark so we came down to the bottom of that mountain. We spent that night in one of the very, very old abandoned houses there. I am a mature man, but when I was small I cannot sleep in very old houses, because of the scare and because of the fearness. But if you are in that situation, and you get the opportunity to sleep in that kind of an old house, you enjoy your sleep very much. Because we were homeless, we had to sleep in that house and it was a good sleep.

We woke up early that morning and fed at the mountain that we had just crossed. If you look at that mountain it is beyond our imagination that we had crossed it. That mountain is quite steep and high. It's all foggy. We have crossed that mountain but we don't know how we have crossed that mountain.

Again we have continued our journey. It was very difficult to walk because of the fog and because of the cold. And the air was difficult. In our group some people wanted to go this way and some of the people in our group wanted to go in another direction. We had a little bit of arguments. Some of the monks in our group are totally exhausted. They don't want to cross another mountain. They decided to go on the road of the Chinese trucks and the Nepalese border police. Once you walk on the streets somebody will surely catch you and put you in prison because you are trying to escape Tibet. Some of the monks in our group decided to go in that direction.

Some of the people in our group, including myself, encouraged them by reminding them of the twenty days it took us to cross the huge Himalayan mountains and the other mountain. Now we only have a few more distances to cross through mountains and then we will be in India. We had a discussion and tried to encourage those monks. Suddenly

one of the monks from our group, named Anchoe, disappeared. We were all trying to look for him. We don't know
what happened to him. We don't know whether he died or
whether he is alive. He just disappeared suddenly. We were
shouting his name..."Anchoe," because there was a very
thick forest and foggy weather. We can't see him because of
the fog. We shout his name but he never answered back. We
don't know what has happened to his life. We heard shouts
by some children and we knew there was a family near, so
we proceeded towards that family.

We saw one small path. We saw some small footprints
and some big footprints on that path. We followed that path.
Finally we reached the place where we spent another night.
We met two people. They were a man and a small child we
recognized because we met them earlier somewhere. That
man and child had some food and we requested them to save
some of their food for us because again we are running out
of our food. The man decided to sell us a pack of tsampa. We
paid him thirty Nepalese rupees and bought a pack of tsampa from him. Half of the tsampa we left there for him. Then
we could see small paths on the mountain. We followed that
small path and crossed the mountain again and we reached
the backside of the mountain. All this time it was raining.

And in the rain there are small leeches that suck your
blood. Our legs were full of leeches and sucking our blood on
that mountain. Wherever we walked, we don't know how,
they attacked us. Our bodies were full of leeches and they
were sucking our blood, especially on the nerves. They stuck
on nerves like a magnet and they suck your blood away.
Since they are stuck on your nerves it's difficult to pull them
off. The best way is to use salt. If you put salt on your body
then that helps and the leeches drop off.

That night we spent together and also with that man and
small child. We were eating only tsampa and water and they
were cooking. They brought some potatoes. But they didn't
give us even a piece of potato. As monks we should not steal
their food. We have a strong desire of eating potatoes, but he
didn't give us even a piece of potato in that night. He's also

running out of his food. Since he knows the way of how to cross that mountain we give him forty Chinese currencies as a guide. We requested him to show us the way to cross that mountain and since he's a merchant he knows how to cross that mountain. Finally he showed us and guided us. He showed us the direction to go to India. The worst thing is that we cannot understand his language very well. That's the worst part. But he showed us the direction to go to India and we followed on that direction.

After following in that direction finally there is a small path that splits into two directions. Again we have some problems throughout the monks in our group. They wanted to go to the right and three of us wanted to go to the left. We had some problems again because the one passage goes to a different direction and this passage goes to another direction. We don't have any idea where we are going or where those passages lead us. We are trying to decide.

We have some problems here and some of the monks decided that they don't want to go in that direction. They are ready to follow the other path. We rested and had some tsampa together that belongs to everyone. Afterwards we distributed the tsampa. Each monk got his share of tsampa. There isn't any water around to make the dough so we ate it with the snow. If you eat your tsampa with the snow it becomes very big and that helps you to fill your belly. You make a very big tsampa and eat it. Because we five have been traveling together since Tibet, I told them that we should not split into two groups. We should be one group. It's better because we can help each other if one faces some problems.

Finally those other two monks are very strong and they just don't want to go to the other direction. We all followed these two monks and went in that direction. But that was on the wrong direction. Again we reach a very high mountain and that mountain cannot be crossed. But from the top of that mountain we can see some very old houses made out of bamboo. That night we slept in one of the bamboo houses. And in the night we made a fire in that bamboo house. Since there are many bamboo houses we made a big fire. In that night, unfortunately, one of my friends shoe was also burnt in that fire. When we woke up in the morning one of his shoes is already burned by the fire and he has no shoe.

We tried to go to a different place to see if there is something left behind from the previous group. Fortunately we saw one white pair of shoes that was left from a previous group. The monk used those white shoes. We think that those shoes were given to him by the Three Jewels. This is our belief because it was the right time for him.

From the top of the mountain we could only see the clouds and fog and the trees. But deep in the middle of the forest we can hear some of the voices of the people and the children that were playing and shouting. Because we heard the noise of the children, we moved down the mountain until we reached that small village. We got all of our belongings together and went to one of the families to beg for food. We gave them our torch (flashlight) and other items and they gave us some tsampa. That was also very delicious. And again we continued on our journey.

It took us one complete day to get to the opposite side of the mountain. It was raining heavily and we are hungry and it's difficult. We don't know how to go to India now. If we go in that direction we are not very sure whether we will reach India or not. I was worried and full of regret and suddenly I saw a bunch of sheep sleeping under their shelter. We are in the rain and they are very peaceful. At that time I wished I could be one of the sheep because they were sleeping so peacefully.

It is too late to go back to Tibet now, and it is difficult and very far away, and now we are not going the right direction to India. We had a terrible time. Later on we came across a field that grows corn. We stole some of the corn and ate in the row of corn. There was a small cave that we found. In that cave we slept together – all of my friends in that cave.

The next morning we woke up to find there are many Nepalese and we don't understand any Nepalese and they don't understand any Tibetan. We had a very big problem. What I did was I have one watch and I gave my watch to one of the Nepalese and I tried to get some food from him. He took my watch and gave us food. He gave us potatoes and wheat noodles. That was the most delicious food I had during my entire journey. Even after just having the three big bowls of noodles my stomach is full but my mind is not yet full. We kept eating even after consuming three bowls. Everybody is full and it's sort of hard to walk because you are full. You have just eaten more than three big bowls and you're all full. Everybody is lying down like a pig.

Even though there's another small village on the opposite side, if you go directly it will take only six hours to get to that town. It's a small village called Bhaktapur. But it took us two days for us to reach that small village. We sold our belongings and we bought some food and ate a lot of food and relaxed.

A Nepalese child came up to us and he showed us how to cross the border because there are two different border police and usually they said it is quite difficult to cross the border. That day we prayed. We did the chanting call Ngur–ze–ma. We were praying Ngur–ze–ma. That Nepalese child, he's very smart, he left for a few hours and checked everything at the border. He came back and said that there's nobody at that border. We went straight across the border and got to the other side. As soon as we reached that small village we paid eighteen Nepalese rupees for a big plate of rice. You can eat one or two big plates of rice. It is quite cheap and we ate a lot of rice. The owner of that small restaurant was surprised because we ate three big plates of rice at one time.

We are happy because Katmandu, which is the capital city of Nepal, is quite near and there are many busses going to Katmandu city. We decided to leave some of our old clothes and we had a calculator that we gave to that small child. Then we took a bus from that village to Katmandu. Finally we reached Katmandu. Once we reached Katmandu, the capital city of Nepal, we hear that there is a Tibetan office, which is called the Tibetan Reception Center Office. We directly went to that office and the people there took care of us. They gave us a place to sleep, they gave us food, they gave us clothes,

and they gave us medicine. They are kind and they are helping the refugees.

After spending two weeks in that Reception Center, they
bought us bus tickets from Nepal to India. They put every
one of us in the bus and we reached Delhi, the capital city
of India. From Delhi to Dharamsala, again there are some
Tibetan people who work in the Reception Center in Delhi.
They bought our bus ticket to Dharamsala, where His Holiness the Dalai Lama lives.

We spent one week in Dharamsala. I was with another
twenty-six refugees. One day they gave us the opportunity
to meet His Holiness the Dalai Lama. He shook hands of each
and every refugee and he asked questions like...'where are
you from'...'where would you like to go'...'to school or to
the monastery'...'or some other places'. Nobody was able to
answer because everybody is happy and everybody is crying
and nobody is giving him answers. All the twenty-six people
there were crying. That time I felt a very strange feeling. I
just cannot express that feeling. It is like a small child, when
that small child meets his own mother he has some sort of
extraordinary feeling. When we see His Holiness the Dalai
Lama in real life our heart is so overwhelmed and I just cannot explain or describe that kind of feeling. But it is some
kind of special feeling that I experienced.

Even though it was very hard for me to tell each and every story because I cannot speak out in front of him. Finally
I was able to tell him something about why I escaped Tibet,
the two reasons of my escaping Tibet, and then finally he
advised me to go to the monastery and he advised me to continue my Buddhist Philosophy studies. I can't believe I'm in
front of His Holiness the Dalai Lama. It's like a dream. Still,
I'm kind of like in the air. I don't believe that I'm in front of
him. It's like my dream.

I told His Holiness the Dalai Lama about the people who
are still in Tibet - especially the old people who wish to get
the blessings of His Holiness the Dalai Lama but can't because they are too old or they can't escape Tibet. I told him
about my teacher who's too old to escape Tibet and I re-

quested him to bless my teacher and asked him to pray for all those beings who are suffering. At that time I have some problems with my stomach. I had an ulcer. I told him about my ulcer. He gave me some medicine that is called Renchen-rinbu. Renchen-rinbu means "precious pills." It helps my ulcer problem. I used half of the pills for myself and I sent half of the pills back to Tibet to my parents.

Then I moved down to the southern part of India to get admission to the monastery - the Gomang Monastery. Even in the monastery I had some problems. We were poor when we got to the monastery. It was real starvation. We had many problems. But since we don't have much time I'm not going to share those problems. Since then I've been practicing and I've been continuing my studies of the Buddhist Philosophies. This is just a brief story.

Interpreter: It was not so brief! (laughter)

It was an amazing story. Thank you. I would also like to know how he was chosen for this group and what does he think of traveling around the country?

In addition to my Buddhist Philosophies studies, I also work for the monastery. For the last fifteen/sixteen years I've been learning Buddhist Philosophies at Gomang Monastery. But in the monastery each and everybody has a responsibility. We all have a duty to perform. A few years ago, for about six months, I spent six months as a teacher to look after the students who came from Mongolia. Not from Mongolia, Russia, the other Mongolia. I spent six months as their teacher at Dharamsala. I've been working for the monastery since then.

For the last three years I was elected as one of the administrators for the whole monastery. Also this year I finished the master's degree in Buddhist Philosophies and obtained my Geshe degree. Some of the officers in the head office requested me to join this group, because for the last three years

I've been working very hard for the monastery and I've been taking the full responsibilities on my shoulders. They asked me to take part in this group too. I obtained my degree and had some time and I agreed to do this. That's why I was chosen for this group.

The second reason is that I heard America was a very big country and a very powerful country. One of my younger brothers lives in New York City and has been living in this country for the last few years. I thought that it is a good opportunity for me to see such a big country and experience something new. At the same time I can meet my brother in New York City.

When I got to this country I had the opportunity to call my parents on the phone for the first time since I left my parents. I was able to talk to them on the phone because it's cheap and it's very easy to call from here to China (from here to Tibet) rather than from India to Tibet.

When I talked on the telephone to my father, he told me that twenty days after I left he became very worried about me. He was distraught for twenty days – crying and thinking of me because my father didn't know whether I was alive or not. My father got the message from the monastery that I didn't come back to the monastery. Because I had told a lie to the monastery and had lied to my parents. My father told me that for the twenty days he did not sleep in his house. For the twenty days he was roaming here and there – crying and praying for me. My father did special prayers for me. My father, my teacher, and my other relatives, they did special prayers for me. My parents still hope that one day we will meet each other. But my teacher, who was very old when I left Tibet, he was already dead. He is no more on this earth. But my parents still hope that one day we can meet each other. This is about all what I can share with you.

*   *   *   *

We found out about two months after this interview that Geshe Lobsang Kunga received the sad news that his mother passed away.

Shakya Tenzin

My name is Tenzin. My name means "those people who preserve Buddha's teaching." I was born in Tibet at Kham sometime in 1969; however, I'm not sure of the date. I have a big family. I have two brothers and three sisters. My family still lives in Tibet.

My family is Nomad and Farmer mixed. During the summer my mother and one of the children go to the mountains with the animals. My father and the rest of the family stay home and work in the field. I am the only monk in the family and I am the youngest child. When I was young I worked in the fields. And also I go with the animals. But during the summer I go to the mountains and stay with the animals. I became a monk when I was fifteen.

You studied in Tibet?

No, I couldn't get the opportunity to study in Tibet. I escaped Tibet in 1983 and then I went to Nepal first. I stayed there almost two years. I start studying in Nepal.

Could you tell us a little bit about how you escaped and made it to Nepal? Where you with other people?

Yes, there were three of us. First, my plan was to go to Lhasa in Central Tibet. I planned to join the monastery in Lhasa. But when I arrived in Lhasa they have some problems there. You know. Some political problems. And people from outside Lhasa cannot stay longer than a week. So we had to leave. I thought, okay…there is no reason to go back home. Then I decide to go to India and study Tibetan culture and religion.

So you were with two friends?

Yes.

What was it like trying to cross the border? Did you encounter any of the Chinese soldiers? Did you have any great difficulties?

Yes, it was really difficult because I walked all the way from home to Nepal. It took almost two and a half months. And between the Lhasa and Tibetan border there's a lot of Chinese military. We cannot go on the main road. We always have to go around the mountains and we have to hide. We mostly journey through the night.

Were there people along the way who told you how to get to Nepal?

Yes…some people…yes.

Did they take you in and feed you and help you?

Yes. You know, I have this small backpack for food. But it's empty and I have to go to some village and ask them if I can have some tsampa and these things. Yes, those people are good and they give me lots of tsampa, butter, and cheese... these things.

Did you have any close calls with the Chinese? Did they ever stop and question you or anything?

I met one Chinese, but he was not a policeman or soldier. I don't know his position, but he asked me where are you going, why you coming here? I say I am going to visit the Holy Place. You know, there are lots of Holy Places, such as Milarepa Cave. Milarepa is known for meditating for many years. I told him I'm going there.

Did you cross the Himalayas?

Yes. I had to cross on foot. When I escaped Tibet it was winter. There's a lot of snow. I crossed the Himalayan Mountain – Mt. Everest. But I didn't go on top.

You went around Mt. Everest.

Yes. Mt. Everest was like this and I go through here. *(He demonstrates with his hands.)*

So you were with you two companions when you did this?

Yes.

You had enough food and water to make that journey?

Yes, but we had very little food. And we don't have money.

We had to beg. Sometimes we go to a Tibetan village. They would give us tsampa or something else to eat.

When you made it to Nepal were there people there that helped you get to India? Or did you have to walk from Nepal to India?

No. I took the bus. When I got to Nepal, the first time I went to a Boudhanath. Boudhanath means huge stupa. Thousands and thousands of years old stupa. The Tibetan people live around this stupa. They go to it every day and they make circumbulations and prostrations. There I met some Tibetans. They showed me one of the Tibetan reception places in Katmandu and they took me to the reception place. The reception place is run by the Tibetan Government-in-Exile. I stayed there for one week and they gave me food and clothes.

Were you a monk at this time?

No.

You become a monk when you went to India?

No. At the Tibetan Reception Center they asked me what I wanted to do. You have the choice where you want to go. If you want to go to school you can go. If you want to go to the monastery you can go. So they can help. I chose to go to monastery. There's a small monastery that I went to.

Is being a monk something you had hoped to be most of your life? As a young man did you want to be a monk?

Yes.

Did your family study Buddhism in Tibet?

They are Buddhist but they did not study. There's no chance to study.

Backtracking here...all of the monks have told us about their escape from Tibet. How do you find your way out of Tibet? Did you have to travel at night? How did you know the correct direction so that you weren't wandering around the mountains?

Actually, we don't know the exact directions. There was a small path. We go on that path. Sometimes we get lost for one day, and we go back again and again through that path. Very difficult. During the day we climb on the mountain and we sleep. And we looked out on the road and watched.

Once you made it to India and went to the monastery, what was the name of that monastery?

Drepung Gomang Monastery. I have been there almost seventeen years now.

You've been studying Buddhism and English. What else did you study there?

The main thing I studied was Buddhist Philosophy. I tried to study English but it's difficult. I live in the monastery and the monastery has rules and regulations. I have to go through all this. There's no chance to study English.

How did you learn English?

In 1997 I took the vacation from the monastery and I went to North India to Dharamsala and I studied English there.

So you did it all on your own, pretty much?

Yes.

Are you studying to become a Geshe?

Yes. I graduated from all my classes so I can take Geshe exam now.

Is this your second or third trip to the United States?

Third.

How were you originally chosen to be a part of the tour group?

In 1999 Drepung Gomang Monastery chose me to be Administrator. We have eight Administrators. I speak a little bit of English. We divide the jobs. The tour is kind of my job. Since 1999 then I come with the tour.

Is part of your job organizing where you will be going?

Yes.

What was your first impression when you came to America and suddenly you saw computers and TV's and cars everywhere and all the wealth? What were your thoughts about that?

I thought, "How could they make things like this?" It's very, very techno everything. But now I am used to it. I use a computer and communicate through the Internet with my friends in India and America. All this I learn from America.

What do you enjoy most about traveling around with the tour group and what are some things maybe don't like so much. I guess you must get homesick for your family?

Oh yes. Yes, I mostly enjoy when we reach the school, university, college, or high school and sometimes we make the sand mandala and we talk about Tibetan culture and the current situation of Tibet. The young students they are really interested and they ask many different questions. They are curious about Tibetan history. This is good.

How do you feel now that this is your third trip? You feel that being out in the public like this you think it's helping as far as helping Americans to better understand the Tibetan cause?

Yes, this is really good! Because we are helping each other to benefit one other.

Do you see an improvement in the spirituality of the people you're coming across, as far as...

Yes, I think usually American people, or most American people, are spiritual. But lots of people don't know how to study. They really like the spiritual life. But they don't know how to study.

Are they accepting of Buddhism? Do you find most people accept Buddhism and see the benefits of it?

Yes.

During the early Sixties we have read that some Tibetan Buddhists were reluctant to teach Buddhism to the Westerners because they felt we weren't disciplined enough or that we weren't ready, or capable of practicing. What do you think changed that and what do you think is the state of Buddhism in America today?

We're thinking all the countries have their own religions. We believe that it's better to study one's own religion. We always say when we talk about Tibetan religions, that if you are really interested you can study. But we never try to convert people to Buddhism. They study a little bit and then some people lose their own religion and they sometimes cannot understand Buddhism. So…I don't know for sure. We do know that a lot people study Tibetan Buddhism and they are really good practitioners.

This group recently performed at Carnegie Hall, which is a world famous performance hall. What were your impressions of being there and being a part of that event?

I think it was quite interesting and really good because this concert was for the benefit of Tibet. So that's what I like. The people who made the music, rock-n-roll, was really loud.

Do you enjoy that kind of music?

It's too loud.

What about last Saturday when you performed with the American Indians at Ft. Ancient? What were your impressions of that event?

I feel really good. It was peaceful and very good.

Was there a familiarity about their music as being similar to Tibetan music as far as the drumming or anything?

Yes. Some chanting is similar to Tibetan chanting.

You've been traveling for three years and you're the most experienced traveler of this touring group. Have you any especially funny stories you would like to share with us of your travels here? Anything when you think of a moment or an event that you want to tell us about?

The most funny thing was during the tour last year when we went to New York. The tour group got up very early one morning and we drove a long time to Nantucket. We went to Nantucket and we made a sand mandala. The next morning when we woke up two monks cooked. We always take turns. They woke up and tried to make some Tibetan butter tea. Then one of the monks, he is quite funny, he put some butter in the pot and put it on the stove. Then they fell back to sleep. The butter is burned and the smokes come out. Then the fire alarm sounds. It was really loud, like it's a police car giving sound, similar like that. Two monks and I are asleep in other rooms. One minute later everybody is just do-do-do-do (running about). The mother, the American lady, she had two kids and she thought maybe it's a fire and she took the baby and ran outside. Then I come into the kitchen and tried to put out the fire. Two or three minutes after police come.

Is there anything you want to say about Tibet or about how we can help Tibetans or Tibet?

Yes. To help Tibet the most important thing is to know the situation and truth about what is happening in Tibet and to the people there. So if people know the truth and can help, this will be very good.

Tenzin Tenkyong
(Dorje)

*M*y name is Tenzin Tenkyong. I am called Dorje.

Does your name have a meaning in your language?

Tenzin means 'the one who respects or the one who preserves the Dharma properly'. That means Tenzin. The practitioners keep the Dharma properly. The meaning of Tenkyong is 'the one who benefits all the practitioners' or 'the one who holds the Dharma properly.' And Dorje means 'thunderbolt.' What we call Vajra is Dorje. So this is the wisdom. And also it symbolizes the unconditional or unchangeable wisdom.

Beautiful! Can you tell us where and when you were born?

I was born in 1976 in the month of April in the Northern part of India. Near the Himalayas in a village called Amanali.

Do Tibetans celebrate their birthdays?

No. Most of the Tibetans don't celebrate. But we accept His Holiness the Dalai Lama. We celebrate the birthday of His Holiness the Dalai Lama and very other high lamas like the Panchen Lama. But now the lay society of young Tibetans who are parents, they do celebrate their children's birthdays.

Can you tell us a little bit about your family, if you have brothers or sisters, what business your family was in?

My family members are farmers. I have four brothers. I am the only monk in the family.

When did you feel the calling to become a monk? How old were you?

I was nine years old. I went to live and study at the Drepung Gomang Monastery when I was nine. I have been there for sixteen years studying Buddhist philosophy. I also work in the library. There is a computer master in the library and I enjoy computers very much. I also practice the experiences I have learned from the Buddhist philosophies.

Did you study English at the monastery?

Yes, from Gomang School. In the monastery we have a small school from one to eighth grade. In that small school we learn English, Tibetan History, Tibetan Languages, and also Social Studies and some General Science.

***Can you tell us a little bit about an average day, what it's
like to live in a monastery so when people read the book they
can get a feel for what a monk's day is like...?***

*(Topten (the interpreter) discussed this with Dorje and they
decide that Topten should explain it.)*

I think it's easier if I tell you how their day starts and their
day ends. I think most of the monks, generally speaking,
wake up at six o'clock in the morning. They get breakfast
- usually a cup of tea and piece of bread from the common
kitchen. The Elder monks, as soon as they wake up, they do
some prostrations in front of the shrine room or altar room.
And also some of the teachers, what they do, most of the
teachers try to do some meditation for half an hour or for
maybe one hour. After that, as a teacher in the monastery,
we don't have classrooms or something like that. What they
do is all the students they go to the teacher's room just to receive the teachings from the teacher for about a few hours.

Then at nine-thirty in the morning the gong starts and
they go to the debate session from nine-thirty. They debate
until eleven. In that debate session all the students must go
and at the same time all the teachers will go to the debate
session to help out the monks. The main purpose of debate
(and also in Tibetan Buddhist society) is to create the mis-
conception in order to establish the correct view based on the
subjects or texts. They debate on different kinds of subjects.
Like how one should try to generate compassion or reach the
compassion...how one can find the compassion. And also on
how one can meditate on reality of nature, impermanence,
all this kind of Buddhist Philosophies stuff. The debate is one
of the most important ways of learning the Buddhist Philosophies.

They get lunch at eleven o'clock. From eleven to twelve
it's lunchtime. Since our monastery is situated in the Southern part of India, during the summer season it's too hot during the noontime to have classes. The temperature goes way

beyond forty-seven degrees Celsius. That's more than one hundred degrees here. So it's hot. During the raining season, since our monastery is situated in a remote area in the Southern part of India, the rain is just terrible. When it rains it rains throughout the day, throughout the night. Sometimes it just keeps raining one week throughout the days and nights. That's why it is quite difficult for monks to continue their studies during the noontime. As soon as they finish their lunch some monks get to take nap until two.

Some monks go to attend their teachings. Once again they go to the different teachers' rooms and get the teachings from them. And then again at five o'clock they get their supper or dinner from the common kitchen. Most of the time they get the noodle soup that you have been enjoying because that's easy to make. Because the kitchen has to supply food for fifteen hundred monks you can imagine how difficult for the cook to prepare food for the fifteen hundred people at the same time. From five to six it is the supper or dinnertime.

Then from six again there are some students who go to attend the teachings. And at six-thirty most of the monks will go to the debate ground to continue their debate with their teachers. From six-thirty onwards they will debate until eleven. And sometimes if the weather is good, if it is not too hot, or not too cold, or if it not raining, some of the very studious monks they do debate until midnight. The younger monks go to school and come back to their room at eight-thirty in the night. As soon as they come back again they have to memorize and recite whole texts.

In the monastery this is kind of like one day. This is six days in a week, so they have only one day as a weekend. That day is Monday. On Monday they go to meet their friends. They go to the vegetable market to buy vegetables and some monks go and have fun time with their friends. And some monks wash their clothes. Because we don't have washing machines or something like that, they wash their clothes; they clean up their rooms and all these things. This is pretty much a day in the monastery.

Let's talk a little bit about this tour group...how you were selected for this tour group.

I have been to different countries in Europe with the same tour group as last year I am experienced at making the mandalas and many of the different activities. That is why the monastery chose me to continue on the culture tour with this group.

I noticed when you were worked on the mandala you would sit there for six, seven hours straight.

Yes, yes.

Everyone else would get up and go and you were still there. Do you find great pleasure in working on the mandala? Is it meditative for you? How do you feel about doing this?

There is a saying that the practice makes man perfect. So if through the practices I can just concentrate my mind only on the sand mandala. And then I can also concentrate my mind on all the energy of the mandalas that help my body to be relaxed. That's why I can sit down and continue pouring the sands for more than six hours at one time.

It's hard for Westerners to understand this. You create this beautiful piece of art and when you're finished you usually wipe it away. Can you explain a little bit why you do that?

As soon as we complete the sand mandala we usually sweep it up or we just destroy it. The main purpose behind the destruction of the sand mandala is that it's a lesson to each and every one of us that all the things and humans came into being with the causes and conditions and also even intrinsic existence. It's also giving us a lesson that the moment changes. It changes every time. Nothing remains there permanently. Even when we finish the mandala, it was perfect, beautiful - it's an amazing piece of art, like a masterpiece. But we destroy it because it gives us reason to overcome our attachment.

If you are too attached to that kind of beautiful object or material object, then here it is nothing. There is nothing there. There is not any permanence there. It is a lesson of the impermanence and to try to overcome the attachment to the materials or whatever it may be. It is a lesson to each and every one of us to remind that one day, we are like sand mandala and one day our causes and conditions will destroy our lives. So we should not have the strong feeling of attachment towards the materialism, the things and events, having the nature of impermanence.

You're also very involved with the music. Is there a special thing about the music that you do? Is there a specialty or thing that you enjoy most about making the music?

I'm a specialist in drumming.

Drumming? So you must have really enjoyed being with the Americans Indians making music on Saturday.

I enjoyed playing with the Natives - especially when we were drumming. I really enjoyed that. I appreciate each and every one of them that they are trying to preserve their very ancient culture that has been gradually vanishing away from this earth. They are preserving their culture. Like Tibetans we are also trying to preserve our culture that has been vanishing and being deliberately destroyed by the Communist Chinese Government since 1959. I enjoyed my time with them.

Do you have any impressions of America you would like to share with us?

I heard it's a big country and also it is a very developed

country. And people are enjoying so much of material developments and material possessions. I don't know whether they have the real peace in their mind and heart, because we cannot judge from the outside. It seems that they are happy with all their material possession, but at the same time I don't know whether they are happy with their mind - their inner mind - and heart.

What do you enjoy most about being with the group and is there anything maybe you don't enjoy so much?

It is quite difficult being with a group sometimes because we go to different places. Sometimes we experience different weather, the climate, and the bad conditions. For example: in this week if we are in a hot weather maybe next week we could go to some other place where there is rain or cold. It is quite difficult for me to adjust to that kind of climate conditions. But at the same time I'm doing my best. I'm working hard, along with the monks, to bring the peace, and to share our culture, in order to tell other people how peace is important on this earth. I'm trying my best, along with my group. Most of the time I'm quite happy with my group.

What will you do once you return to India? Will you continue to study? Do you wish to be a Geshe?

Yes, as soon as I finish this tour group I will return to India to continue my studies. And also I would like to improve my computer skills that might help the monastery in order to preserve all the ancient texts and reproduce it in booklet forms. I'm looking forward to that.

Did that interest come from working in the library?

Yes, working in the library I feel very happy. I enjoy working in the library because I can read many different kinds of books. I can read very old books and try to re-edit each and try to type it in a computer and reprint. I enjoy working in the library.

Have you had the opportunity to meet the Dalai Lama? And if you did, were you inspired by him?

When I first became a monk I take refuge from His Holiness the Dalai Lama. My name was given to me by His Holiness the Dalai Lama. I think that I am quite lucky. He advised me and also other monks and other children who become a monk at the same time. He advised us and that inspired us to continue our studies in the monastery.

Is there any message you would like to give to the people who read this book? Anything that you would like to say as far as what they might be able to do to help Tibet?

I would like to request all of the readers to support Tibet and Tibetan peoples struggling for their independence, struggling for their freedom. Also I request all the readers and all the people of the world to try to support the Tibetan people in order preserve this very ancient culture and support Tibetan people in order to prevail the blissful peace on earth.

Geshe Lobsang Tsetan

My name is Geshe Lobsang Tsetan. Geshe means 'teacher.' Lobsang means 'good heart.' And Tsetan means 'long life' and also 'the life without much hurdles or sufferings.'

Could you tell us where you were born and when you were born?

I was born in the northern part of India – one of the Himalayan regions... Ladakh – in a small village called Doshkosh. I was born in the year 1966, May 15th. My family is a very big family. I have one older brother and three sisters. And the rest of the five brothers are younger brothers.

Are any of them monks?

Yes, including myself, and my youngest brother, he is a monk in the southern part of India in the same monastery.

Were your parents farmers?

Yes, they are farmers.

Do you get to see them very often, your family?

When I first got admission to the monastery I didn't see my parents for maybe six years. That was in 1979. Then after 1979 I've been able to go back to the northern part of India and meet with my parents quite often.

Did you feel a calling to become a monk?

I became a monk at the age of seven. One of my uncles and one of my grandfathers... they were monks. In our village there was a small monastery that is called Garshen Monastery. I spent about five to six years in that monastery.

Maybe you can tell us what's involved to become a Geshe. What you had to do to become a Geshe.

I studied my Buddhist philosophy teachings in the year 1981. I had to study the Buddhist philosophies for the last twenty years to obtain the Geshe degree, which is the PhD degree in Buddhist philosophy. I obtained the Geshe Lharampa degree in the year 2000. In the Buddhist schools we have different level of classes. The first two basic classes are elementary classes called Dhurah. We have to study for two years on those classes.

There is another class called Pramana that is called the Pramana School. In that school I had to spend three years learning all the texts of the Pramana. After that I was four or five years in the school called the Prajnaparimita School. Then I spent two years in the Middle Way or Madhyamika School. I studied about six years in the school of the Abhidharma and the Vinaya schools. At the same time I studied for the big monastery examination called the Gelugpa examination in order to obtain the PhD degree in Buddhist Philosophies. I spent six years studying the Gelugpa examinations in order to secure that degree in Buddhist Philosophies. After obtaining the Geshe degree in the year 2000, I went to the northern part of India to the Tantra school. I was there one year learning the Tantric tradition of Buddhist Philosophies.

Do you continue to study and are there other levels that you reach with your furthered studies and do you intend to do that?

Yes, I would like to continue my studies when I return to India because this is the mission in my life. Until now I have been just passing through all those different classes. Now it's time to learn or to continue or to place importance on the Tantric teachings. I have a keen interest in learning more about the things that are taught through the Tantric tradition.

Even though I have obtained the PhD degree in Buddhist Philosophies, as I compare my degree to those monks who obtained, or used to obtain, the PhD degree in Tibet, each is about sixty years old. Because in the monastery it is not just something you study and try to obtain in order get a good job or to become famous. To them to obtain the higher degree means to learn something more. To go deeper into the Buddhist Philosophies is the goal.

That's why those monks who were in Tibet took so many years to obtain the PhD degree. When they achieve that degree they are over sixty or sixty-five. Even though I have already obtained that degree, I would like to continue my studies, as I have mentioned before, in the Tantric tradition of the Buddhist teachings. In the world of the Twenty-first Century everybody is busy and things happen quite instantaneously. It is like that even in the monastery. Most of the monks want to become Geshes at a very young age. That is not the case. To obtain the Geshe degree means to study more in the Buddhist Philosophies. That is why I would like to continue my studies.

Do you want to continue to study for the sake of the knowledge you will gain or do you want to eventually teach others what you have learned?

Yes. My main mission for continuing my studies is to benefit others or to teach others...to share my knowledge with others. When I get back to India I don't have to go to the debate session since I have already finished all those classes. There will be many monk students who will come to me and try to receive the teachings. My main aim is to share my knowledge or to teach my knowledge to the monks while practicing and continuing my own studies.

In addition to that, since we think that the teachings of the Dharma, the Buddhist teachings, are precious and important, that it is the responsibility of each and everyone of us to preserve them and try to give it away to someone through whom they can also teach or other sentient beings or other human beings. That is the reason why I would like to continue my studies. If I think about my own sake then the studies that I have done or the experiences that I have is quite enough. But it's not enough when it comes to giving the correct view to others.

By joining the tour group you're with now, have you found that the teachings you shared have been worthwhile on your trip?

The main aim of this culture tour is to try to share the Buddhist teaching qualities and also to bring the messages of the peace and harmony that are taught in the Buddhist philosophies. That is the main mission of this culture tour. I would say that it is quite worthwhile. We have been visiting different high schools, colleges, and universities. Last week we were at Columbia University in Missouri and a couple of months before we were in New Jersey and New York City visiting high schools.

When we talk about the Buddhist teachings it helps and benefits the school or college students. I would say it was a worthwhile of benefit to those people who seek the Buddhist teachings on how to overcome all the daily obstructions and daily sufferings and in order to prevail the peace in their minds and the other peoples.

But I have been telling the students of the high schools and the universities that they should not come and believe in the Buddhist way of teachings. Rather they should do some experiments and observations before they jump on the Buddhist teachings. Most of the time when I talk in the colleges, the high schools, and the universities, I'm talking about how one should generate compassion and loving kindness. How one should use the human intellectual wisdom in a positive way that benefits other beings, society, or community. One should try to work, in a constructive way, not to use intellectual capability in a destructive way. This is quite common.

And I'm also telling them about the precious life of human body and human intellect. Whenever I talk in front of the high schools and the colleges, after the talk we always have discussions or questions and answers. There are many students who gain interest in the teachings in the talk and they ask many different kinds of interesting questions. It is doing something for the students. I would say that it is quite worthwhile.

I think that it is very important to me and my own responsibility to teach them something very good that might help them. Because the students are like a bud on a flower before it blooms out. Once they finish their studies they are like flowers that bloom out. When they are like a bud it is important to teach them or to give them all the virtuous quality activities when they finish their school. As they bloom out, they bloom out with a very beautiful mind and heart so that will benefit them.

Have you had a chance to measure how spirituality is in the Unites States...the state of spirituality in the West?

As far as I'm concerned I think that, especially people in the United States (because I have already been to European countries), as I compare the people of this country and compare the people of the different Asian countries, the people who are here in this country are more open and they participate in different kinds of religions. They participate in learning from different philosophies and different religions. But if you compare this to the Asian people, most of the Asian people do not participate in different kinds of religions. Whatever they believe or whatever they follow, they follow one religion. Here most of the people, as far as what I have experienced, they try to learn each and every philosophies of the different religions. I would say that their spirituality status is very good and they are open-minded.

I have a deeper question about the spirituality of Mankind throughout our world. Are you hopeful that we can rise above the terrible violent things that are happening? Are you hopeful that through people studying any religion, be it Buddhism or whatever, is there some way we can rise up and be better?

I hope and I believe that those people who practice any kind of religion, whether they practice the Buddhist teachings or any other religion... it doesn't matter. I think that one day, if they study on one particular thing quite seriously, and once they achieve a certain level; they can also do some good things to preserve peace and to overcome all those violent activities. I would say one day it will happen.

I have a question about karma. We heard you speaking of karma the other night. About how you create your own karma and how it affects what happens to you when you return to live another life. I've been thinking a lot about the people of Tibet and the terrible things that have been happening to

them. Is that the result of karma?

I agree with your point that even in our society we always talk about karma and when we talk about karma we are also talking about the karma of each and every individual, which is called the collective karma - the karma that has been accumulated together. Our society has its own karma. It is like that. The Tibetan people are suffering, dying, and having many problems under the Communist Chinese Government. Most of the Tibetan people and practitioners think that it was their karma or their cause from a previous life. That it was their karma.

You mentioned accumulative karma or karma of a group of people, as in the case of China perhaps, is it accumulative karma within that country that is going to keep causing the problems within Tibet? I guess national karma is the word I'm looking for.

Here when we talk about the group karma we have to go back and read the history of Tibet. At some point the Tibetan people and Tibetan government did some things that should not have been done. Those are the negative karma. Now that negative karma has the result and suffering of the Tibetan people right now like the loss of our country and all these sufferings are the result of that karma. But there is an end for that kind of group karma because here if you see this generation of Tibetan people in India, in exile, we have our Tibetan government. And the people who work in the Tibetan government are very sincere. They are very good and working hard to get our country back or to look after the refugees who are escaping or coming back from Tibet. Now that group karma has been accumulated by the different people in a right way. One day we hope and we believe that the karma we are laying down these days will have a definite result. And that result you can describe as the day when we will get our country back with the help and support of the people of the world.

I have a question about reincarnation. I find it a very appeal-
ing thought and I wanted to know if you are aware of any of
your previous lives, and if so, does that awareness help you
to be any better or more compassionate a person...and the
third part of the question is...is it possible for someone like
me to be become aware of my previous states?

I don't have any knowledge nor am I aware of my previous
life. But when I look into my present human form then I can
surely say that my previous life would have been in human
realms. In order to be reborn in this human form you should
have a very good life in your previous life. It is quite difficult
to tell you if my previous life was as a monk or lay person,
or whatever it may be. It is quite difficult to distinguish that.
But I can say that through my own experiences and experiments, my previous life was also in the human realms.

In Tibetan society there is a saying that your intellectual
status when you are small contains a combination of the intellectual status of your previous life experiences and it can
be recognized. That's why, when I was small, my parents
would tell us stories of Tibet and the Tibetan people. Or when
I saw monks I had a feeling of becoming a monk or going to
Tibet. I always felt a very strange feeling in my heart. That
shows that there is a connection. But I cannot say this is exactly right. Something is there.

Your present body is a result of previous causes from
your previous life. You have accumulated some good karma
or good causes in your previous life. That is why you are
enjoying results or actions of that previous good karma now.
Once we know or have the clear understanding of the law of
causality or the law of karma one can say that the present
body or the present realm is a result of the previous realms.
One can say that because you are in a human realm you
have accumulated very good actions in your previous life.

I think that in my previous life I didn't practice too much
generosity or giving because when I first went down to the
southern part of India to get admission to the monastery, the
whole monastery was very poor and the monastery did not

have any food to give to the monks. When I first took admission into the monastery, my admission number was one hundred eighty two. That meant that there were already one hundred eighty one monks in the monastery. The monastery at that time was very small and very poor. In the morning we only got a cup of tea...no bread or no tsampa. For lunch we only get a small portion of bread and that bread had to be shared between three monks. We also got a cup of tea but no vegetables. For dinner we had a bowl of rice with a few beans...very few beans...mostly water.

We have been getting this kind of food until 1988. Then in 1988 the monastery was able to find some sponsors and through their help they were able to open a carpet factory. Through that carpet factory they are able to buy vegetables for the monks. They were able to open the carpet factory with assistance. After a few years the income that was been generated in the carpet factory helped the monastery to buy the bread to give to the monks for breakfast.

These days, as you know, we have fifteen hundred monks. The food is not too good, but it is okay. In the morning we get bread and tea and also for lunch, rice and vegetables, and sometimes we get bread with the vegetables. But, compared to the food they are enjoying with the other families, this is still very simple food. That's why the monks don't get good food and they have to study outdoors and do not have good sanitation facilities. That is why many of the monks get sick. There are still many sick monks up there in the monastery. The monks who are older than us have worse problems. They had problems with starvation because at that time, in the 1960's and 1970's, the monks had just escaped Tibet and they had a big problem.

In closing, is there any message you would like to share with the readers of the book that would help them and Tibet as well?

I don't have any special things or special messages for the readers. But I would like everyone to remember the stories of the monks. Though my story, as compared to the other monks, is not as terrible because I didn't face any harsh events in my life. Most of the monks escaped Tibet and as you know they had terrible sufferings on the way of escaping. I would like to request each and every reader of this book to read it seriously and to also see the injustice of the Tibetan people and the truth of the Tibetan people. And I would like to request them to support Tibet and the Tibetan people in order to get our country back from the Red Communist Chinese Government. This is all I could say. Thank you.

Thank you, Geshe Tsetan, for sharing your knowledge and insights with us. You are very kind.

"*If we have a good heart, a warm heart, warm feelings, we will be happy and satisfied ourselves, and our friends will experience a friendly and peaceful atmosphere as well. This can be achieved nation to nation, country to country, continent to continent.*"

His Holiness the 14th Dalai Lama

An Overview of Buddhism

It's not our purpose in this book to explain Buddhism and its teachings. There are many excellent books that give detailed information about Buddhism, His Holiness the Dalai Lama, Tibet, meditation and more. However, we felt it would be appropriate to offer a very general overview for those of you who are just learning about Buddhism through your contact with a tour group or members of the Buddhist community.

The foremost reasons for following the teachings of Buddha are to be free from suffering and to find happiness. The fundamental teachings to help us achieve these goals are known as the Four Noble Truths. These were the first teachings of Buddha after he had attained enlightenment.

The first of the Four Noble Truths is knowing the EXIS-TENCE OF SUFFERING. Buddha taught that suffering inter-fuses our lives on a daily basis and it therefore affects our bodies and our minds. Understanding this we are able to see that we are not happy all the time and that suffering is part of our reality. Acceptance of this fact will allow us to not dwell on the negative aspects of our lives.

Once we understand the first Noble Truth we can move on to the next Noble Truth of looking at the CAUSES OF SUFFERING. Buddha taught that the causes of suffering are desire and attachment. Humans are always wanting some-thing they don't have (physical or emotional) or believing they lack something in their lives or desiring that something that does not exist in their lives. Even desiring that which is good (such as world peace or good health for a friend) can lead to suffering as we cannot always affect outcomes.

The Third Noble Truth is that of CESSATION OF THE CAUSES OF SUFFERING. The basis of this Noble Truth is that once we know the cause of the suffering, we can achieve its cessation. This can be done by ending the cause of the suf-fering.

Finally, the Fourth Noble Truth shows us the PATH TO THE CESSATION OF THE CAUSES OF SUFFERING. Called the Noble Eightfold Path, these guidelines for living show us how to free ourselves from desire and attachment and how to end our suffering. Once we reach this point, we have found nir-vana.

The Noble Eightfold Path is taught as being divided into three groups:

I: Morality – One must have 'right speech', 'right action' and 'right livelihood'.

II: Concentration – One must have 'right concen-tration', 'right mindfulness' and 'right effort'.

III: Wisdom – One must have 'right understand-ing' and 'right thought'.

The Buddha in his teachings simplified the Four Noble Truths for his students in this way. He described them as medicine for someone who is sick. He first realizes that he is sick. Next he knows he must find out what is making him ill. Thirdly, he must believe that he can become well. And, finally, he must take the medicine necessary for his good health to return.

Love Is The Universal Religion

And, as His Holiness the Dalai Lama has expressed many times in his talks and books, we need to understand that peace and happiness will come to all if we treat each other with love and respect. If we do nothing else, try not to harm anyone or anything we come in contact with. The result will be a better world for all (humans and animals).

"We are what we think.
All that we are arises with our thoughts.
With our thoughts we make the world."

Buddha

Glossary of Terms

Bardo: Intermediate state between death and the next rebirth or another of the transitional states of experience.

Bodhi: Enlightenment. Derived from the root 'buddh', meaning "to awaken". This term in Buddhism denotes the perfect realization of the truth which causes the cycle of transmigration to end and brings about nirvana.

Bodhichitta: The enlightened mind which altruistically acts in the interest of all beings, combining discriminative awareness with compassion.

Bodhisattva: A spiritual trainee who has generated the altruistic mind of enlightenment and is on the path to full Buddhahood, remaining in the world in order to eliminate the sufferings of others.

Buddha: Meaning "Awakened One." Epithet of Shakyamuni.

Buddha Shakyamuni: The historical Buddha known prior to his attainment of Buddhahood as Siddhartha or Gautama, who is also revered as the fourth of the thousand Buddhas of this aeon. He is depicted in diverse forms - seated, standing, or reclining, and with diverse hand gestures.

Chakpurs: Metal funnels used to disperse colored sand for the painting of mandalas.

Chuba: Tibetan national dress tied at the waist with a sash. For men it takes the form of a long-sleeved coat and for women a long dress with or without sleeves, which may be shaped or shapeless.

Dalai Lama: Revered as the human embodiment of Avalokiteshvara – the patron deity of Tibet who symbolizes compassion. The successive Dalai Lamas have, since the mid 17th century, assumed both spiritual and temporal authority in Tibet.

Dharma: The theory or practice of the Buddhist doctrine, including its texts and transmissions.

Dorje: Thunderbolt or wisdom.

Drokpa: Nomad.

Drubkhang: Meditation hermitage.

Drung: Story.

Dukhang: The assembly hall of a large monastery, in which the monks affiliated to the various colleges will congregate.

Dzogchen: Great perfection.

Eight Auspicious Symbols: Umbrella, fish, conch, eternal knot, vase, wheel, flower, and victory banner.

Emptiness: The absence of inherent existence and self-identity with respect to all phenomena, the ultimate reality underlying all phenomenal appearances.

Gelukpa: An indigenous school of Tibetan Buddhism, founded in the 14th century by Tsongkhapa, which, from the 17th century onwards, came to dominate the spiritual life of Tibet and Mongolia.

Geshe: A teacher. After more than 20 years of extensive studies in Pramana, Madyamika, Abhidharma and other related subjects, a monk is eligible to appear before the Gelugpa Examination Board. After finishing that he will be honored with the highly venerated Geshe Degree (equivalent to the Doctorate of Philosophy in Western University).

Greater Vehicle: The system or vehicle of Buddhism prevailing in Tibet, Mongolia, China, Korea and Japan, emphasizing the attainment of complete liberation of all sentient beings from obscurations and sufferings.

Guru: Spiritual teacher.

Hinayana: The 'small vehicle' in which the practitioner concentrates on basic meditation practice and an understanding of basic Buddhist doctrines such as the Four Noble Truths.

Incarnation: The human form taken by an incarnate lama following his decease in a previous life.

Karma: Recompense for one's actions, entailing a series of transmigrations and rebirths from which both Hindus and Buddhists try to free themselves through their religious practices. According to the doctrine of cause and effect, our present experience is a product of previous actions and volitions, and future conditions depend on what we do in the present.

Kumbum: A stupa containing many thousands of images and often multiple chapels, also known as 'Tashi Gomang' stupa.

Kunga: Popular or likeable.

Lama: Spiritual mentor or guru venerated by his students, since he is an authentic embodiment of the Buddhist teachings. As spiritual authority, he can be the head of one or several monasteries and possess political influence. There are three ways one can become a Lama. The first is by having this title bestowed on one by his or her students. The second way is for a teacher to complete a three year retreat. Once one comes out of this retreat, they are honored with the title 'lama'. The third way is if one is recognized as the incarnation of a passed lama. One will also be given the title/name 'Rinpoche' as well. Lama Thubten Zopa Rinpoche is a good example of this.

Lamrim: The graduated path to enlightenment and the texts expounding this path.

Lesser Vehicle: The system or vehicle of Buddhism prevalent in Sri Lanka, Thailand and Burma, emphasizing the four truths and related teachings through which an individual seeks his own salvation, rather than the elimination of others' suffering..

Lobsang: Good heart or good soul.

Losar: Official Tibetan New Year held at the beginning of the first month of the lunar calendar, which normally falls within February or early March.

Lungta: Tibetan mantras printed on cloth for use as prayer flags, which are activated by the power of the wind, or on paper as an offering to local mountain divinities, in which case they are tossed into the air in a mountain pass.

Mahayana: "Great Vehicle". A school of thought that developed in India around the beginning of the common era as a reaction against the conservatism of the Hinayana Schools. The Mahayana emphasizes the emptiness of all phenomena, compassion and the acknowledgment of Univeral Buddha-nature. The ideal figure of the Mahayana is the Bodhisattva; hence it is often referred to as the Bodhisattva Path.

Madhyamaka: The philosophical system of Mahayana Buddhism based on the Middle Way, which seeks to comprehend, either by means of syllogistic reasoning or by 'reductio ad absurdum,' the emptiness or absence of inherent existence with respect to all phenomena. A distinction is drawn between the ultimate truth, or emptiness, and the relative truth in which all appearances exist conventionally.

Mandala: A symbolic two or three-dimensional representation of the palace of a given meditational deity that is of crucial importance during the generation stage of meditation.

Mantra: A means of protecting the mind from mundane influences through the recitation of incantations associated with various meditational deities, thereby transforming mundane speech into Buddha-speech.

Momo: A Tibetan dumpling.

Monk: One who maintains the full range of monastic vows as designated in the Vinaya texts.

Ngawang: Powerful speech.

Nectar: The ambrosia of the gods which grants immortality. Metaphorically identified with the Buddhist teachings.

Nirvana: Extinction or the destruction of desire and suffering. Nirvana ends the cycle of transmigration. It is the goal of spiritual practice in all branches of Buddhism. It requires completely overcoming the three unwholesome roots – desire, hatred and delusion – and ending active volition. It means freedom from the determining effect of karma.

Paljor: The wealth.

Pandita: Scholar, a Buddhist scholar of ancient India.

Phowa: A meditations practice in which one prepares his 'mind' or 'consciousness' to leave the body at the time of death. This meditation form is practiced by students within the Nyingma lineage of Tibetan Buddhism. If one masters this practice during his lifetime, at the time of death he will be able to eject his consciousness or mind to a chosen Buddha realm – thus attaining enlightenment and becoming a Buddha.

Pilgrim's Circuit: A circumambulatory walkway around a shrine or temple, along which pilgrims will walk in a clockwise direction.

Prajna: Transcendental knowledge or wisdom. The definitive moment of prajna is insight into emptiness which is the true nature of reality. The realization of prajna is often equated with the attainment of enlightenment and is one of the essential marks of Buddhahood.

Prayer Flag: A flag printed with sacred mantra syllables and prayers, the power of which is activated by the wind.

Prayer Wheel: A large fixed wheel or small handheld wheel containing sacred mantra syllables and prayers, the power of which is activated by the spinning motion of the wheel.

Puja: An offering ceremony.

Rinpoche: meaning 'precious jewel'. A Rinpoche is an actual incarnation of a previous (passed) master/teacher/lama. The only people who receive the name/title Rinpoche are those who are recognized as incarnations of these passed masters/teachers/lamas. Not all lamas are Rinpoches and not all Rinpoches are lamas.

Rongpa: Villager.

Samsara: Sanskrit term for transmigration, the cycle of re-births conditioned by karma. Nirvana is the deliverance from samsara or the cycle of existence.

Sand Mandala: A two-dimensional representation of the palace of a given meditational deity, made of finely ground colored powders or sands.

Sangha: The Buddhist monastic community consisting of monks, nuns, lay men and lay women.

Shakti: Energy or power inherent in the female consort of the Hindu deity Shiva.

Shakya: One who follows the path of Buddha's teachings.

Shunyata: Emptiness, according to Mahayana Buddhism a description of the ultimate nature of reality.

Stupa: The most well-known type of sacred monument in the Buddhist world, symbolizing the Buddha-body of reality and holding the relics of the Buddha or some great spiritual master.

Tangka: Tibetan painted scroll.

Tantra: The continuum from ignorance to enlightenment. It is also a highly advanced meditation practice in Buddhism where, if mastered and successful, one can attain enlightenment in one lifetime. The great Tibetan Saint Milarepa is an example of this.

Tara: The female bodhisattva of compassion. There are several forms of Tara (red, white, green, and of course, the famous Twenty-One Emanations of Tara). The word 'Tara' is Sanskrit for 'she who ferries across'. Tara is swift in aiding those who need assistance along their path to enlightenment/liberation.

Tashi: Good luck.

Tenzin: One who keeps the dharma.

Thukpa: Soup, usually noodle soup.

Vajra: The indestructible reality of Buddha-hood, a scepter-like ritual object symbolizing this indestructible reality.

Torma: Ritual offering cake.

Tsampa: The staple Tibetan food consisting of ground and roasted barley flour, which is mixed with tea as a dough.

Tsetan: Long life without much suffering.

Vihara: A large Buddhist temple.

Vinaya: The rules of Buddhist monastic discipline, the texts outlining these rules.

Zen: Japanese form of Chan Buddhism. Introduced into Japan in the ninth century, it was not formally recognized as a school until some centuries later. More than any other school, Zen stress the primary importance of the enlightenment experience and teaches the practice of zazen – sitting as the shortest, but also the steepest way to awaking.

THE TRUE MEANING OF LIFE

By His Holiness the 14th Dalai Lama

"We are visitors on this planet,

We are here for ninety or one hundred years at the very most,

During that period,

We must try to do something good, something useful, with our lives.

If you contribute to other people's happiness, you will find the true goal,

The true meaning of life."

ABOUT THE AUTHOR

Scott 'Belmo' Belmer is a graduate of South Da-
kota State University with a Bachelors of Science
degree in History and Education. He is the author
of ten books and an avid photographer. Belmo
and his wife Terri live in Northern Kentucky.

Herbs and other natural health products and information are often available at natural food stores or metaphysical bookstores. If you cannot find what you need locally, you can contact one of the following sources of supply.

Sources of Supply:

The following companies have an extensive selection of useful products and a long track-record of fulfillment. They have natural body care, aromatherapy, flower essences, crystals and tumbled stones, homeopathy, herbal products, vitamins and supplements, videos, books, audio tapes, candles, incense and bulk herbs, teas, massage tools and products and numerous alternative health items across a wide range of categories.

WHOLESALE:

Wholesale suppliers sell to stores and practitioners, not to individual consumers buying for their own personal use. Individual consumers should contact the RETAIL supplier listed below. Wholesale accounts should contact with business name, resale number or practitioner license in order to obtain a wholesale catalog and set up an account.

Lotus Light Enterprises, Inc.
PO Box 1008 TOW
Silver Lake, WI 53170 USA
262 889 8501 (phone)
262 889 8591 (fax)
800 548 3824 (toll free order line)

RETAIL:

Retail suppliers provide products by mail order direct to consumers for their personal use. Stores or practitioners should contact the wholesale supplier listed above.

Internatural
PO Box 489 TOW
Twin Lakes, WI 53181 USA
800 643 4221 (toll free order line)
262 889 8581 office phone
EMAIL: internatural@internatural.com
WEB SITE: www.internatural.com

Web site includes an extensive annotated catalog of more than 14,000 items that can be ordered "on line" for your convenience 24 hours a day, 7 days a week.

The Tibetan Book of Healing
by Dr. Lobsang Rapgay

"Dr. Lobsang Rapgay is one of the foremost Tibetan doctors in the world today and is also a psychologist. *The Tibetan Book of Healing* contains many helpful practices, going into diet, herbs and meditation and providing a number of methods and techniques to follow for self-healing purposes. It contains a wealth of information that will make the book a constant companion for those really seeking to improve their state of well-being."

Dr. David Frawley, author of *Ayurvedic Healing: A Comprehensive Guide*

"Having been the religious secretary to H.H. Dalai Lama and a monk, perhaps the greatest potency in this book is the clear and well laid-out approach for developing a well-grounded spirituality and meditation practice that he (Dr. Rapgay) offers in accordance with body/mind types and which people of all traditions can heartily embrace..."

Bob Sachs, author of *Health for Life, Secrets of Tibetan Ayurveda*

Trade Paper   ISBN 0-910261-40-7   201 pp   pb $12.95

Tibetan Healing Handbook
A Practical Manual for Diagnosing, Treating, and Healing with Natural Tibetan Medicine
by Thomas Dunkenberger

Tibetan Healing Handbook discusses the fundamental principles of health and causes of disease. These include non-visible forces and biorhythmic-planetary influences; classic Tibetan forms of diagnosis, the foremost of which are pulse and urine examination; advice on behavior and healing approaches to dietary habits, as well as the accessory therapeutic possibilities of oil massages, moxabustion, hydrotherapy, humoral excretion procedures and much more.

This book will inform you about the essential correlations and approaches taken by the Tibetan science of healing. It describes the entire spectrum of application possibilities for those who want to study Tibetan medicine and use it for treatment purposes. At the same time, it provides information about holistic remedies so that interested readers can take action to restore their inner harmony and health.

Trade Paper   ISBN 0-914955-66-7   240 pp   pb $15.95

Available at bookstores and natural food stores nationwide or order your copy directly by sending price of item plus $2.50 shipping/handling ($.75 s/h for each additional copy ordered at the same time) to:

Lotus Press, PO Box 325, Dept. TOW, Twin Lakes, WI 53181 USA
toll free order line: 800 824 6396 office phone: 262 889 8561
office fax: 262 889 2461 email: lotuspress@lotuspress.com
web site: www.lotuspress.com

Lotus Press is the publisher of a wide range of books and software in the field of alternative health, including Ayurveda, Chinese medicine, herbology, aromatherapy, Reiki and energetic healing modalities. Request our free book catalog.